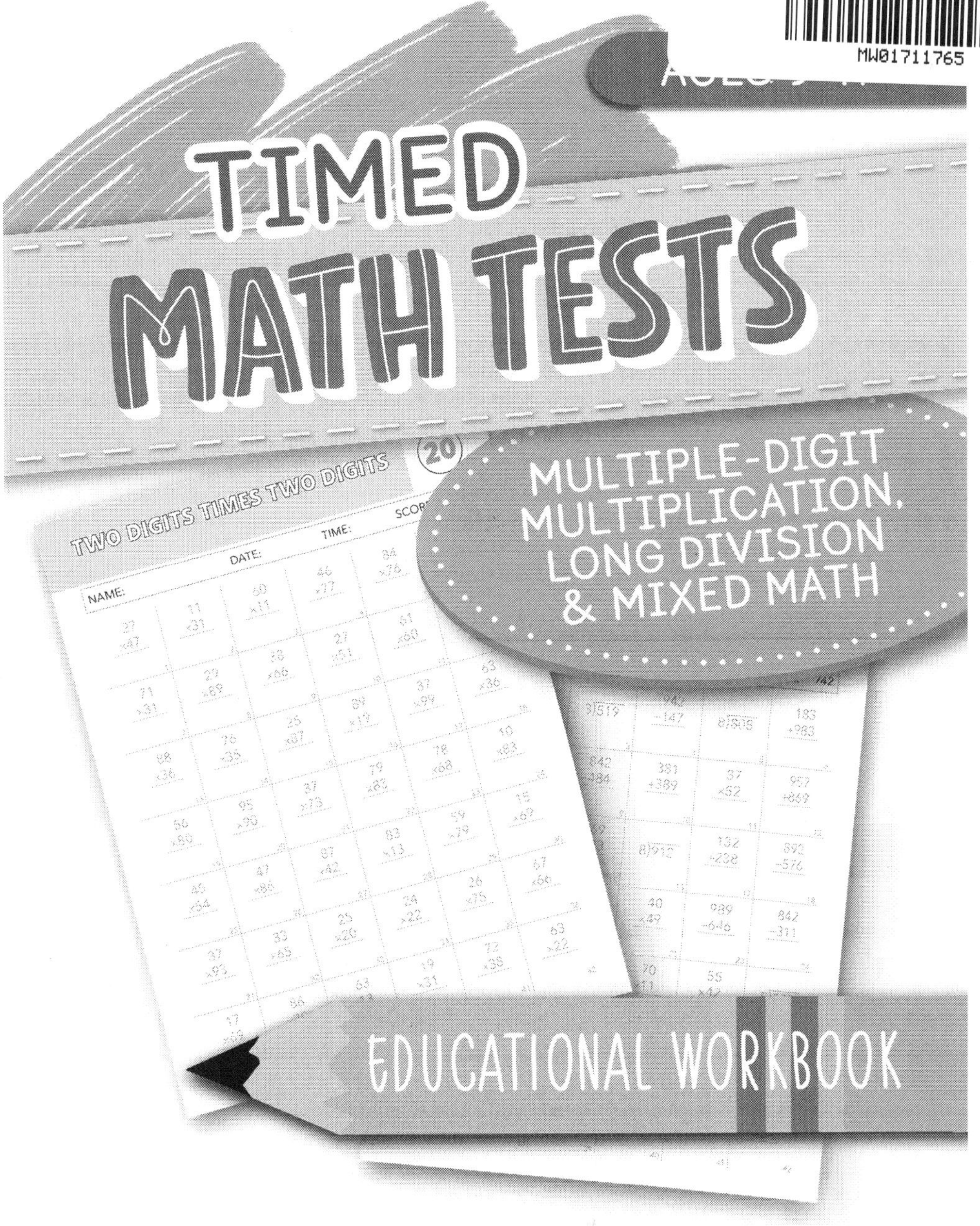

This Book Belongs to:

FOR A LITTLE INSPIRATION
follow along at:

@JUNEANDLUCY

@JUNEANDLUCY

WWW.JUNELUCY.COM

Love free goodies? Join our newsletter by emailing us at **freebies@junelucy.com** to receive freebies, discounts and sales info. Let us know which book you bought by putting the book title in the subject line of your email.

Shop our other books at
www.junelucy.com

For questions and customer service, email us at
support@junelucy.com

INTRODUCTION

Early math skills mastered at a young age provide a foundation for children from their formative years through adulthood. An early understanding of numbers and math sets kids up for greater success in future schooling. Not to mention, math appears to us everywhere – from patterns we see in nature to the change returned from a dollar bill.

With this book, we hope to provide hours of math drills that help kids become proficient in math fluency and retention at an appropriate skill level. When students sit down to practice timed math drills, they are honing their speed and problem solving, skills that they will take with them in the years ahead.

TIPS FOR THIS BOOK:

- The tests start out at a basic level and increase in difficulty. Your student may choose to complete them in the order provided or hop around to test various skills.
- Each test has a handy label indicating the skills tested on that page.
- Many of the problems can be easily solved in the space provided, however as the problems increase in difficulty, kids may need additional room. Keep some scratch paper handy to allow your student all the necessary space to solve the problems.
- Set up a stopwatch or phone timer at the child's workspace to allow them to time their tests OR allow the student to complete them at their leisure.
- Answers to the tests are in the back of the book, allowing you or your child to double check their work.

1 TWO-DIGIT MULTIPLICATION

NAME: DATE: TIME: SCORE: /42

56 × 4 (1)	43 × 9 (2)	29 × 3 (3)	28 × 8 (4)	13 × 8 (5)	77 × 4 (6)
95 × 4 (7)	14 × 9 (8)	42 × 3 (9)	33 × 8 (10)	20 × 1 (11)	42 × 8 (12)
16 × 8 (13)	18 × 6 (14)	34 × 5 (15)	49 × 8 (16)	56 × 2 (17)	71 × 0 (18)
51 × 9 (19)	12 × 6 (20)	71 × 6 (21)	40 × 9 (22)	42 × 7 (23)	95 × 3 (24)
31 × 0 (25)	26 × 3 (26)	22 × 7 (27)	28 × 7 (28)	84 × 7 (29)	62 × 2 (30)
31 × 2 (31)	75 × 8 (32)	42 × 9 (33)	91 × 9 (34)	30 × 1 (35)	53 × 6 (36)
56 × 6 (37)	18 × 8 (38)	85 × 9 (39)	16 × 4 (40)	78 × 9 (41)	69 × 6 (42)

TWO-DIGIT MULTIPLICATION

2

NAME:	DATE:	TIME:	SCORE: /42

44 × 7 1	31 × 5 2	21 × 1 3	65 × 5 4	20 × 5 5	66 × 7 6
99 × 0 7	50 × 4 8	22 × 9 9	91 × 3 10	18 × 9 11	14 × 8 12
88 × 6 13	95 × 5 14	31 × 0 15	28 × 8 16	68 × 8 17	53 × 7 18
26 × 0 19	65 × 9 20	38 × 4 21	12 × 0 22	38 × 2 23	14 × 0 24
55 × 2 25	28 × 4 26	10 × 1 27	75 × 8 28	24 × 6 29	40 × 7 30
19 × 5 31	85 × 8 32	25 × 7 33	82 × 1 34	59 × 5 35	42 × 8 36
51 × 6 37	34 × 7 38	88 × 9 39	64 × 3 40	75 × 0 41	53 × 1 42

3 TWO-DIGIT MULTIPLICATION

NAME:	DATE:	TIME:	SCORE: /42

88 × 5 (1)	78 × 9 (2)	39 × 9 (3)	38 × 2 (4)	64 × 7 (5)	46 × 3 (6)
93 × 1 (7)	61 × 5 (8)	88 × 8 (9)	49 × 0 (10)	53 × 0 (11)	17 × 4 (12)
54 × 9 (13)	82 × 3 (14)	99 × 8 (15)	74 × 8 (16)	56 × 0 (17)	72 × 6 (18)
82 × 2 (19)	68 × 0 (20)	10 × 3 (21)	69 × 3 (22)	73 × 6 (23)	26 × 5 (24)
86 × 9 (25)	30 × 0 (26)	83 × 3 (27)	74 × 3 (28)	57 × 2 (29)	84 × 0 (30)
74 × 1 (31)	40 × 7 (32)	80 × 5 (33)	67 × 7 (34)	45 × 3 (35)	43 × 2 (36)
17 × 3 (37)	51 × 8 (38)	24 × 4 (39)	72 × 1 (40)	33 × 8 (41)	56 × 2 (42)

TWO-DIGIT MULTIPLICATION

4

NAME:	DATE:	TIME:	SCORE: /42

85 × 2 (1)	73 × 0 (2)	17 × 1 (3)	97 × 2 (4)	62 × 7 (5)	74 × 2 (6)
63 × 6 (7)	55 × 2 (8)	52 × 5 (9)	48 × 6 (10)	85 × 0 (11)	79 × 9 (12)
30 × 7 (13)	50 × 3 (14)	62 × 4 (15)	21 × 8 (16)	32 × 4 (17)	59 × 2 (18)
49 × 7 (19)	48 × 8 (20)	78 × 9 (21)	59 × 8 (22)	69 × 6 (23)	35 × 6 (24)
52 × 6 (25)	84 × 5 (26)	10 × 6 (27)	33 × 4 (28)	61 × 9 (29)	53 × 2 (30)
14 × 3 (31)	60 × 0 (32)	22 × 8 (33)	85 × 8 (34)	31 × 7 (35)	46 × 5 (36)
17 × 5 (37)	55 × 9 (38)	48 × 4 (39)	19 × 4 (40)	68 × 8 (41)	38 × 4 (42)

5 TWO-DIGIT MULTIPLICATION

NAME: DATE: TIME: SCORE: /42

76 × 4 1	15 × 3 2	76 × 7 3	86 × 1 4	45 × 4 5	23 × 7 6
33 × 5 7	66 × 9 8	64 × 4 9	67 × 1 10	80 × 1 11	53 × 1 12
27 × 7 13	83 × 3 14	68 × 1 15	30 × 0 16	71 × 6 17	31 × 0 18
85 × 7 19	37 × 0 20	35 × 6 21	89 × 7 22	52 × 5 23	75 × 8 24
75 × 6 25	54 × 7 26	75 × 0 27	69 × 4 28	22 × 7 29	64 × 3 30
55 × 0 31	93 × 6 32	91 × 8 33	64 × 7 34	50 × 8 35	26 × 6 36
17 × 8 37	96 × 2 38	39 × 7 39	45 × 0 40	74 × 8 41	26 × 5 42

THREE-DIGIT MULTIPLICATION

6

NAME: DATE: TIME: SCORE: /42

981 × 1 (1)	896 × 2 (2)	512 × 2 (3)	859 × 5 (4)	511 × 1 (5)	794 × 6 (6)
975 × 3 (7)	489 × 9 (8)	949 × 8 (9)	401 × 6 (10)	600 × 0 (11)	515 × 3 (12)
215 × 6 (13)	509 × 6 (14)	807 × 5 (15)	256 × 4 (16)	199 × 8 (17)	639 × 2 (18)
598 × 9 (19)	469 × 2 (20)	173 × 3 (21)	297 × 8 (22)	917 × 8 (23)	794 × 0 (24)
168 × 0 (25)	434 × 6 (26)	420 × 2 (27)	560 × 1 (28)	699 × 7 (29)	976 × 6 (30)
210 × 2 (31)	724 × 4 (32)	311 × 1 (33)	788 × 7 (34)	757 × 0 (35)	794 × 7 (36)
482 × 1 (37)	711 × 7 (38)	270 × 2 (39)	862 × 9 (40)	213 × 7 (41)	525 × 5 (42)

7

THREE-DIGIT MULTIPLICATION

NAME: DATE: TIME: SCORE: /42

705 × 9 (1)	781 × 4 (2)	868 × 4 (3)	379 × 6 (4)	257 × 5 (5)	931 × 5 (6)
930 × 0 (7)	460 × 2 (8)	859 × 6 (9)	991 × 0 (10)	503 × 9 (11)	608 × 8 (12)
519 × 9 (13)	399 × 3 (14)	995 × 7 (15)	890 × 6 (16)	841 × 0 (17)	348 × 0 (18)
139 × 6 (19)	484 × 3 (20)	618 × 2 (21)	113 × 6 (22)	816 × 6 (23)	870 × 5 (24)
729 × 8 (25)	272 × 9 (26)	774 × 5 (27)	580 × 9 (28)	770 × 8 (29)	650 × 3 (30)
363 × 0 (31)	175 × 9 (32)	792 × 0 (33)	164 × 6 (34)	716 × 6 (35)	694 × 8 (36)
380 × 6 (37)	545 × 6 (38)	150 × 7 (39)	103 × 1 (40)	414 × 4 (41)	528 × 3 (42)

THREE-DIGIT MULTIPLICATION

8

NAME:	DATE:	TIME:	SCORE: /42

392 × 3 (1)	882 × 6 (2)	817 × 6 (3)	180 × 1 (4)	659 × 3 (5)	371 × 9 (6)
522 × 5 (7)	117 × 4 (8)	223 × 8 (9)	220 × 8 (10)	688 × 1 (11)	174 × 7 (12)
849 × 5 (13)	926 × 1 (14)	488 × 3 (15)	706 × 9 (16)	121 × 2 (17)	461 × 5 (18)
393 × 7 (19)	699 × 1 (20)	357 × 8 (21)	913 × 1 (22)	924 × 7 (23)	880 × 8 (24)
545 × 5 (25)	210 × 6 (26)	549 × 3 (27)	509 × 2 (28)	626 × 9 (29)	758 × 3 (30)
310 × 0 (31)	500 × 6 (32)	334 × 5 (33)	182 × 4 (34)	442 × 2 (35)	799 × 2 (36)
927 × 2 (37)	498 × 8 (38)	477 × 4 (39)	535 × 1 (40)	417 × 4 (41)	232 × 8 (42)

9 THREE-DIGIT MULTIPLICATION

NAME: DATE: TIME: SCORE: /42

199 × 8 (1)	448 × 4 (2)	713 × 6 (3)	791 × 9 (4)	510 × 3 (5)	711 × 9 (6)
656 × 2 (7)	736 × 7 (8)	925 × 1 (9)	832 × 5 (10)	804 × 6 (11)	923 × 3 (12)
945 × 1 (13)	932 × 8 (14)	726 × 3 (15)	685 × 3 (16)	110 × 1 (17)	943 × 2 (18)
166 × 4 (19)	832 × 6 (20)	977 × 6 (21)	523 × 1 (22)	588 × 5 (23)	731 × 8 (24)
493 × 0 (25)	257 × 9 (26)	844 × 6 (27)	750 × 4 (28)	635 × 9 (29)	757 × 9 (30)
521 × 5 (31)	414 × 3 (32)	158 × 9 (33)	518 × 1 (34)	809 × 9 (35)	607 × 2 (36)
472 × 0 (37)	678 × 6 (38)	885 × 8 (39)	710 × 2 (40)	217 × 7 (41)	514 × 3 (42)

THREE-DIGIT MULTIPLICATION

10

NAME:	DATE:	TIME:	SCORE: /42

792 × 4 1	238 × 1 2	244 × 4 3	125 × 4 4	798 × 1 5	264 × 5 6
828 × 3 7	215 × 6 8	364 × 4 9	669 × 8 10	807 × 8 11	952 × 0 12
525 × 6 13	452 × 0 14	904 × 2 15	595 × 0 16	441 × 7 17	844 × 2 18
944 × 9 19	594 × 9 20	286 × 9 21	101 × 3 22	987 × 7 23	930 × 2 24
749 × 0 25	447 × 8 26	473 × 9 27	148 × 1 28	951 × 1 29	407 × 9 30
739 × 1 31	920 × 8 32	957 × 5 33	594 × 6 34	257 × 5 35	543 × 6 36
893 × 5 37	375 × 3 38	640 × 6 39	764 × 9 40	647 × 6 41	542 × 7 42

11 THREE-DIGIT MULTIPLICATION

NAME: DATE: TIME: SCORE: /42

293 × 0 1	990 × 7 2	880 × 5 3	176 × 0 4	838 × 7 5	638 × 0 6
781 × 8 7	320 × 2 8	763 × 4 9	114 × 8 10	451 × 6 11	972 × 2 12
736 × 6 13	267 × 4 14	902 × 7 15	973 × 0 16	723 × 3 17	598 × 7 18
351 × 5 19	862 × 9 20	185 × 3 21	382 × 5 22	213 × 7 23	445 × 2 24
771 × 1 25	789 × 1 26	721 × 1 27	867 × 6 28	610 × 3 29	201 × 5 30
204 × 8 31	186 × 0 32	991 × 7 33	970 × 8 34	590 × 0 35	759 × 5 36
136 × 5 37	468 × 0 38	389 × 6 39	713 × 8 40	531 × 4 41	317 × 3 42

THREE-DIGIT MULTIPLICATION

12

NAME: DATE: TIME: SCORE: /42

776 × 4 1	376 × 7 2	583 × 7 3	900 × 6 4	882 × 4 5	538 × 9 6
919 × 9 7	173 × 5 8	567 × 0 9	109 × 7 10	587 × 9 11	999 × 1 12
621 × 7 13	108 × 3 14	254 × 2 15	138 × 3 16	303 × 9 17	153 × 5 18
296 × 3 19	556 × 1 20	926 × 8 21	677 × 6 22	818 × 0 23	482 × 4 24
492 × 6 25	481 × 8 26	281 × 9 27	345 × 1 28	907 × 3 29	971 × 8 30
759 × 8 31	933 × 9 32	783 × 6 33	924 × 1 34	913 × 8 35	375 × 1 36
739 × 9 37	979 × 7 38	593 × 0 39	719 × 6 40	820 × 8 41	539 × 4 42

13 THREE-DIGIT MULTIPLICATION

NAME: DATE: TIME: SCORE: /42

396 × 6 (1)	870 × 8 (2)	610 × 3 (3)	735 × 4 (4)	324 × 6 (5)	817 × 2 (6)
785 × 9 (7)	442 × 4 (8)	726 × 4 (9)	958 × 5 (10)	193 × 2 (11)	657 × 6 (12)
410 × 0 (13)	202 × 8 (14)	927 × 3 (15)	220 × 0 (16)	703 × 9 (17)	656 × 7 (18)
382 × 8 (19)	991 × 5 (20)	617 × 7 (21)	830 × 5 (22)	215 × 5 (23)	649 × 0 (24)
402 × 3 (25)	722 × 7 (26)	491 × 3 (27)	931 × 5 (28)	760 × 8 (29)	629 × 9 (30)
328 × 9 (31)	793 × 5 (32)	748 × 1 (33)	306 × 0 (34)	669 × 7 (35)	258 × 3 (36)
175 × 8 (37)	489 × 3 (38)	671 × 8 (39)	812 × 3 (40)	716 × 5 (41)	622 × 6 (42)

THREE-DIGIT MULTIPLICATION

14

NAME: DATE: TIME: SCORE: /42

309 × 5 1	402 × 5 2	543 × 4 3	690 × 4 4	575 × 5 5	964 × 0 6
902 × 0 7	732 × 7 8	393 × 8 9	968 × 7 10	874 × 7 11	818 × 0 12
453 × 1 13	446 × 0 14	713 × 0 15	236 × 2 16	638 × 1 17	106 × 0 18
213 × 7 19	258 × 3 20	716 × 8 21	197 × 2 22	450 × 6 23	416 × 1 24
450 × 2 25	615 × 8 26	201 × 4 27	484 × 9 28	116 × 3 29	659 × 9 30
305 × 8 31	773 × 1 32	184 × 1 33	724 × 5 34	764 × 1 35	901 × 9 36
596 × 9 37	718 × 6 38	336 × 9 39	521 × 9 40	726 × 4 41	617 × 7 42

15 THREE-DIGIT MULTIPLICATION

NAME: DATE: TIME: SCORE: /42

459 × 7 (1)	810 × 5 (2)	337 × 3 (3)	972 × 6 (4)	928 × 9 (5)	835 × 3 (6)
761 × 6 (7)	385 × 5 (8)	754 × 0 (9)	858 × 9 (10)	936 × 1 (11)	979 × 7 (12)
476 × 7 (13)	857 × 8 (14)	954 × 0 (15)	163 × 6 (16)	120 × 8 (17)	626 × 1 (18)
913 × 9 (19)	694 × 4 (20)	820 × 5 (21)	310 × 2 (22)	584 × 5 (23)	736 × 2 (24)
446 × 5 (25)	771 × 4 (26)	724 × 4 (27)	221 × 3 (28)	228 × 2 (29)	556 × 1 (30)
979 × 6 (31)	592 × 5 (32)	396 × 7 (33)	261 × 2 (34)	265 × 3 (35)	546 × 8 (36)
495 × 6 (37)	299 × 3 (38)	289 × 2 (39)	837 × 1 (40)	459 × 5 (41)	632 × 7 (42)

TWO DIGITS TIMES TWO DIGITS

16

NAME:	DATE:	TIME:	SCORE: /42

40 ×56 1	11 ×82 2	48 ×90 3	51 ×72 4	49 ×81 5	22 ×81 6
35 ×36 7	74 ×33 8	30 ×59 9	10 ×25 10	45 ×23 11	38 ×96 12
42 ×97 13	79 ×85 14	66 ×55 15	46 ×88 16	39 ×88 17	99 ×24 18
61 ×54 19	71 ×90 20	78 ×11 21	48 ×39 22	34 ×35 23	53 ×83 24
15 ×28 25	21 ×30 26	74 ×32 27	84 ×84 28	22 ×41 29	55 ×21 30
37 ×81 31	16 ×29 32	51 ×69 33	52 ×10 34	26 ×92 35	54 ×28 36
52 ×78 37	24 ×57 38	67 ×97 39	20 ×34 40	44 ×28 41	12 ×43 42

17 TWO DIGITS TIMES TWO DIGITS

NAME: DATE: TIME: SCORE: /42

27 ×84 1	96 ×58 2	36 ×11 3	44 ×81 4	60 ×64 5	30 ×21 6
54 ×11 7	10 ×54 8	69 ×79 9	28 ×75 10	60 ×67 11	49 ×30 12
53 ×94 13	30 ×12 14	96 ×65 15	45 ×71 16	54 ×41 17	89 ×26 18
77 ×20 19	42 ×67 20	74 ×77 21	56 ×33 22	66 ×26 23	45 ×42 24
18 ×32 25	63 ×70 26	82 ×38 27	70 ×59 28	38 ×74 29	54 ×83 30
48 ×32 31	50 ×36 32	18 ×14 33	18 ×87 34	56 ×94 35	44 ×15 36
83 ×43 37	89 ×34 38	75 ×28 39	79 ×87 40	80 ×78 41	93 ×27 42

TWO DIGITS TIMES TWO DIGITS

18

NAME: DATE: TIME: SCORE: /42

57 ×93 1	89 ×76 2	44 ×68 3	19 ×33 4	23 ×59 5	82 ×76 6
87 ×64 7	77 ×22 8	77 ×61 9	28 ×92 10	92 ×38 11	33 ×35 12
36 ×26 13	45 ×41 14	42 ×34 15	56 ×56 16	10 ×96 17	70 ×54 18
67 ×17 19	10 ×77 20	16 ×52 21	68 ×16 22	34 ×17 23	69 ×22 24
43 ×67 25	88 ×21 26	27 ×76 27	42 ×21 28	14 ×89 29	45 ×49 30
98 ×26 31	49 ×85 32	75 ×17 33	59 ×17 34	91 ×27 35	59 ×59 36
99 ×44 37	43 ×19 38	39 ×26 39	24 ×50 40	32 ×45 41	54 ×30 42

19 TWO DIGITS TIMES TWO DIGITS

NAME: DATE: TIME: SCORE: /42

36 ×51 (1)	26 ×83 (2)	21 ×31 (3)	19 ×12 (4)	62 ×98 (5)	80 ×38 (6)
85 ×47 (7)	46 ×76 (8)	39 ×94 (9)	79 ×85 (10)	53 ×38 (11)	89 ×94 (12)
92 ×41 (13)	45 ×19 (14)	65 ×55 (15)	98 ×88 (16)	25 ×80 (17)	63 ×52 (18)
19 ×51 (19)	11 ×23 (20)	55 ×27 (21)	75 ×37 (22)	51 ×82 (23)	42 ×84 (24)
29 ×51 (25)	31 ×61 (26)	79 ×16 (27)	47 ×47 (28)	71 ×46 (29)	55 ×65 (30)
40 ×96 (31)	62 ×94 (32)	41 ×83 (33)	62 ×62 (34)	44 ×88 (35)	32 ×41 (36)
18 ×79 (37)	15 ×12 (38)	17 ×72 (39)	73 ×76 (40)	37 ×85 (41)	42 ×67 (42)

TWO DIGITS TIMES TWO DIGITS

20

NAME: DATE: TIME: SCORE: /42

27 ×47 1	11 ×31 2	60 ×11 3	46 ×77 4	84 ×76 5	36 ×83 6
71 ×31 7	29 ×89 8	38 ×66 9	27 ×51 10	61 ×60 11	40 ×82 12
88 ×36 13	76 ×35 14	25 ×87 15	89 ×19 16	37 ×99 17	63 ×36 18
56 ×80 19	95 ×90 20	37 ×73 21	79 ×83 22	78 ×68 23	10 ×83 24
45 ×54 25	47 ×86 26	87 ×42 27	83 ×13 28	59 ×79 29	15 ×69 30
37 ×93 31	33 ×65 32	25 ×20 33	24 ×22 34	26 ×75 35	67 ×66 36
17 ×69 37	86 ×70 38	63 ×13 39	19 ×31 40	72 ×38 41	63 ×22 42

21 TWO DIGITS TIMES TWO DIGITS

NAME: DATE: TIME: SCORE: /42

63 ×30 1	61 ×10 2	48 ×50 3	88 ×47 4	89 ×66 5	56 ×13 6
29 ×87 7	61 ×88 8	92 ×63 9	82 ×19 10	62 ×94 11	42 ×19 12
35 ×73 13	45 ×32 14	20 ×80 15	42 ×43 16	30 ×15 17	83 ×38 18
50 ×35 19	76 ×89 20	42 ×92 21	23 ×10 22	88 ×60 23	15 ×54 24
27 ×59 25	66 ×15 26	96 ×86 27	70 ×79 28	43 ×58 29	54 ×76 30
67 ×71 31	51 ×47 32	59 ×87 33	90 ×71 34	82 ×82 35	89 ×11 36
27 ×17 37	66 ×55 38	83 ×21 39	52 ×47 40	67 ×32 41	32 ×24 42

TWO DIGITS TIMES TWO DIGITS

NAME:	DATE:	TIME:	SCORE: /42

88 ×40 (1)	33 ×25 (2)	49 ×33 (3)	42 ×50 (4)	65 ×97 (5)	86 ×20 (6)
44 ×88 (7)	17 ×67 (8)	39 ×27 (9)	12 ×16 (10)	92 ×87 (11)	52 ×30 (12)
83 ×75 (13)	55 ×82 (14)	12 ×99 (15)	25 ×69 (16)	88 ×75 (17)	75 ×48 (18)
92 ×26 (19)	52 ×22 (20)	32 ×38 (21)	79 ×86 (22)	88 ×63 (23)	82 ×24 (24)
87 ×30 (25)	97 ×36 (26)	25 ×60 (27)	63 ×84 (28)	44 ×11 (29)	73 ×58 (30)
80 ×49 (31)	34 ×66 (32)	75 ×38 (33)	90 ×10 (34)	43 ×69 (35)	91 ×55 (36)
26 ×98 (37)	11 ×23 (38)	91 ×10 (39)	81 ×55 (40)	31 ×13 (41)	57 ×62 (42)

23 TWO DIGITS TIMES TWO DIGITS

NAME: DATE: TIME: SCORE: /42

59 ×13 1	44 ×18 2	90 ×48 3	55 ×74 4	57 ×80 5	77 ×12 6
41 ×26 7	76 ×38 8	27 ×50 9	89 ×30 10	25 ×39 11	45 ×28 12
34 ×49 13	53 ×18 14	83 ×77 15	83 ×27 16	44 ×22 17	91 ×51 18
39 ×74 19	79 ×58 20	49 ×55 21	10 ×44 22	21 ×15 23	21 ×42 24
23 ×69 25	25 ×21 26	72 ×89 27	93 ×29 28	22 ×91 29	50 ×25 30
86 ×22 31	70 ×38 32	26 ×73 33	11 ×49 34	51 ×37 35	36 ×54 36
44 ×77 37	44 ×13 38	41 ×78 39	47 ×57 40	38 ×24 41	65 ×16 42

TWO DIGITS TIMES TWO DIGITS

24

NAME: DATE: TIME: SCORE: /42

14 ×51 1	19 ×48 2	67 ×19 3	77 ×92 4	12 ×50 5	28 ×43 6
12 ×60 7	59 ×13 8	20 ×73 9	61 ×42 10	36 ×50 11	24 ×48 12
64 ×40 13	49 ×47 14	73 ×80 15	94 ×64 16	36 ×41 17	45 ×88 18
51 ×97 19	70 ×93 20	31 ×24 21	41 ×65 22	47 ×31 23	29 ×64 24
59 ×59 25	50 ×52 26	31 ×18 27	99 ×67 28	36 ×24 29	78 ×16 30
87 ×27 31	31 ×82 32	13 ×21 33	84 ×78 34	59 ×52 35	44 ×75 36
15 ×25 37	99 ×77 38	32 ×41 39	19 ×90 40	26 ×64 41	67 ×28 42

25 TWO DIGITS TIMES TWO DIGITS

NAME: DATE: TIME: SCORE: /42

60 ×90 1	93 ×14 2	94 ×33 3	63 ×92 4	14 ×61 5	40 ×40 6
91 ×23 7	21 ×36 8	55 ×19 9	44 ×36 10	93 ×37 11	57 ×39 12
85 ×52 13	28 ×50 14	22 ×79 15	52 ×66 16	62 ×99 17	61 ×59 18
58 ×62 19	96 ×33 20	41 ×46 21	85 ×74 22	27 ×24 23	56 ×15 24
61 ×72 25	92 ×98 26	36 ×72 27	53 ×87 28	54 ×85 29	94 ×31 30
25 ×84 31	11 ×56 32	49 ×53 33	44 ×65 34	67 ×19 35	29 ×67 36
21 ×93 37	38 ×33 38	38 ×85 39	70 ×30 40	56 ×18 41	84 ×24 42

DIVISION

NAME: DATE: TIME: SCORE: /42

8)48 1	8)32 2	4)16 3	6)6 4	1)5 5	5)25 6
3)6 7	9)18 8	7)14 9	4)4 10	6)12 11	9)45 12
4)12 13	9)81 14	4)36 15	3)9 16	3)18 17	5)15 18
3)15 19	2)12 20	8)64 21	3)27 22	9)54 23	2)2 24
9)9 25	3)12 26	6)18 27	7)35 28	5)10 29	7)56 30
8)16 31	7)28 32	5)35 33	9)27 34	7)21 35	2)6 36
4)8 37	9)72 38	7)49 39	6)24 40	2)10 41	8)40 42

DIVISION

NAME: DATE: TIME: SCORE: /42

$5\overline{)35}$ 1	$2\overline{)12}$ 2	$3\overline{)6}$ 3	$9\overline{)36}$ 4	$5\overline{)15}$ 5	$3\overline{)18}$ 6
$5\overline{)45}$ 7	$4\overline{)16}$ 8	$2\overline{)6}$ 9	$5\overline{)5}$ 10	$9\overline{)18}$ 11	$9\overline{)63}$ 12
$2\overline{)20}$ 13	$9\overline{)72}$ 14	$6\overline{)6}$ 15	$6\overline{)36}$ 16	$5\overline{)25}$ 17	$5\overline{)20}$ 18
$8\overline{)64}$ 19	$5\overline{)30}$ 20	$4\overline{)24}$ 21	$3\overline{)9}$ 22	$7\overline{)49}$ 23	$8\overline{)16}$ 24
$3\overline{)21}$ 25	$2\overline{)18}$ 26	$6\overline{)24}$ 27	$9\overline{)45}$ 28	$5\overline{)40}$ 29	$8\overline{)24}$ 30
$2\overline{)28}$ 31	$4\overline{)12}$ 32	$6\overline{)18}$ 33	$4\overline{)20}$ 34	$9\overline{)27}$ 35	$6\overline{)54}$ 36
$8\overline{)32}$ 37	$7\overline{)63}$ 38	$6\overline{)48}$ 39	$3\overline{)15}$ 40	$2\overline{)8}$ 41	$7\overline{)56}$ 42

DIVISION

28

NAME: DATE: TIME: SCORE: /42

4)16 1	7)42 2	6)12 3	9)72 4	4)12 5	2)10 6
6)36 7	3)15 8	4)20 9	8)32 10	8)64 11	6)42 12
2)16 13	6)18 14	5)25 15	7)14 16	4)36 17	2)8 18
2)14 19	7)56 20	8)24 21	2)20 22	8)16 23	5)15 24
4)8 25	5)20 26	2)2 27	9)63 28	8)40 29	5)30 30
8)48 31	5)10 32	9)81 33	7)49 34	9)18 35	3)3 36
7)63 37	2)4 38	2)18 39	4)24 40	8)56 41	9)36 42

29

DIVISION

NAME: DATE: TIME: SCORE: /42

3)21 (1)	9)45 (2)	5)5 (3)	3)15 (4)	6)30 (5)	9)18 (6)
7)7 (7)	7)63 (8)	1)3 (9)	4)12 (10)	8)24 (11)	8)48 (12)
5)25 (13)	3)27 (14)	6)6 (15)	9)27 (16)	7)42 (17)	4)32 (18)
5)40 (19)	9)72 (20)	2)16 (21)	8)32 (22)	3)18 (23)	3)3 (24)
6)42 (25)	7)28 (26)	3)6 (27)	5)45 (28)	8)16 (29)	5)10 (30)
2)14 (31)	9)36 (32)	8)72 (33)	5)35 (34)	4)20 (35)	2)6 (36)
6)18 (37)	2)18 (38)	4)28 (39)	7)14 (40)	4)36 (41)	7)21 (42)

DIVISION

30

NAME: DATE: TIME: SCORE: /42

7)35 (1)	9)54 (2)	3)24 (3)	9)36 (4)	3)15 (5)	5)25 (6)
4)32 (7)	5)30 (8)	3)27 (9)	4)12 (10)	3)3 (11)	7)42 (12)
7)21 (13)	5)55 (14)	3)9 (15)	5)45 (16)	6)18 (17)	2)20 (18)
3)12 (19)	9)27 (20)	1)6 (21)	6)54 (22)	2)6 (23)	7)63 (24)
6)6 (25)	7)49 (26)	4)20 (27)	5)35 (28)	8)24 (29)	8)32 (30)
2)4 (31)	5)15 (32)	6)24 (33)	7)28 (34)	5)20 (35)	3)6 (36)
3)21 (37)	6)12 (38)	2)2 (39)	4)4 (40)	4)36 (41)	7)56 (42)

31 DIVISION

NAME: DATE: TIME: SCORE: /42

5)25 1	6)48 2	2)6 3	3)6 4	6)30 5	2)8 6
6)12 7	8)48 8	8)40 9	6)6 10	4)4 11	4)28 12
4)20 13	4)12 14	7)49 15	3)9 16	7)35 17	9)27 18
8)32 19	3)24 20	4)16 21	5)35 22	7)14 23	3)21 24
9)36 25	8)64 26	4)24 27	6)36 28	9)63 29	2)18 30
2)14 31	1)4 32	4)8 33	8)8 34	7)28 35	5)40 36
2)4 37	7)21 38	6)24 39	5)5 40	5)20 41	5)30 42

DIVISION

32

NAME: DATE: TIME: SCORE: /42

9)90 1	2)18 2	8)24 3	6)36 4	3)12 5	5)50 6
1)4 7	2)14 8	9)72 9	6)30 10	9)27 11	9)54 12
3)27 13	5)55 14	8)48 15	5)30 16	7)21 17	3)36 18
4)36 19	8)16 20	8)32 21	2)36 22	3)18 23	4)8 24
2)4 25	8)72 26	3)9 27	7)42 28	9)45 29	8)56 30
9)36 31	6)24 32	8)40 33	7)49 34	5)40 35	3)6 36
2)8 37	9)81 38	5)45 39	3)3 40	2)12 41	9)18 42

33 DIVISION

NAME: DATE: TIME: SCORE: /42

$1\overline{)4}$ 1	$5\overline{)35}$ 2	$3\overline{)12}$ 3	$6\overline{)54}$ 4	$4\overline{)28}$ 5	$3\overline{)9}$ 6
$5\overline{)45}$ 7	$2\overline{)6}$ 8	$7\overline{)42}$ 9	$6\overline{)6}$ 10	$4\overline{)36}$ 11	$8\overline{)8}$ 12
$7\overline{)28}$ 13	$4\overline{)32}$ 14	$9\overline{)54}$ 15	$4\overline{)4}$ 16	$7\overline{)63}$ 17	$9\overline{)9}$ 18
$8\overline{)72}$ 19	$5\overline{)20}$ 20	$2\overline{)24}$ 21	$6\overline{)42}$ 22	$5\overline{)30}$ 23	$8\overline{)16}$ 24
$2\overline{)12}$ 25	$7\overline{)49}$ 26	$8\overline{)32}$ 27	$5\overline{)40}$ 28	$7\overline{)35}$ 29	$8\overline{)64}$ 30
$3\overline{)3}$ 31	$4\overline{)24}$ 32	$6\overline{)30}$ 33	$2\overline{)2}$ 34	$2\overline{)14}$ 35	$7\overline{)56}$ 36
$7\overline{)14}$ 37	$5\overline{)25}$ 38	$8\overline{)48}$ 39	$4\overline{)20}$ 40	$2\overline{)4}$ 41	$5\overline{)15}$ 42

DIVISION

34

NAME: DATE: TIME: SCORE: /42

6)54 1	3)21 2	8)48 3	4)32 4	6)36 5	5)45 6
4)16 7	8)64 8	8)24 9	5)40 10	3)18 11	4)40 12
6)18 13	2)12 14	8)8 15	2)4 16	2)8 17	3)6 18
4)36 19	4)28 20	4)12 21	8)72 22	9)63 23	9)36 24
3)9 25	5)25 26	2)14 27	3)3 28	8)56 29	7)21 30
7)14 31	9)54 32	7)35 33	7)7 34	8)32 35	4)8 36
2)2 37	7)63 38	3)12 39	5)35 40	7)56 41	7)49 42

35

DIVISION

NAME: DATE: TIME: SCORE: /42

6)36 (1)	2)14 (2)	7)35 (3)	9)45 (4)	7)56 (5)	2)12 (6)
3)27 (7)	5)15 (8)	3)18 (9)	7)28 (10)	7)49 (11)	7)14 (12)
6)24 (13)	6)42 (14)	2)6 (15)	3)15 (16)	5)20 (17)	4)28 (18)
5)10 (19)	8)32 (20)	2)8 (21)	9)54 (22)	8)48 (23)	5)30 (24)
8)56 (25)	6)54 (26)	9)27 (27)	3)3 (28)	5)45 (29)	5)35 (30)
4)8 (31)	6)48 (32)	7)77 (33)	7)42 (34)	5)25 (35)	7)21 (36)
7)63 (37)	2)4 (38)	9)9 (39)	8)24 (40)	8)64 (41)	2)10 (42)

TWO AND THREE-DIGIT DIVISION

36

NAME:	DATE:	TIME:	SCORE: /36

7)133 (1)	9)468 (2)	4)104 (3)	5)85 (4)	2)166 (5)	7)420 (6)
7)168 (7)	9)648 (8)	8)600 (9)	5)445 (10)	4)392 (11)	3)60 (12)
3)102 (13)	4)376 (14)	3)108 (15)	3)219 (16)	8)632 (17)	9)657 (18)
5)310 (19)	7)455 (20)	2)32 (21)	8)344 (22)	3)222 (23)	3)138 (24)
3)63 (25)	7)266 (26)	8)432 (27)	5)485 (28)	5)115 (29)	8)416 (30)
3)48 (31)	2)144 (32)	2)52 (33)	5)140 (34)	6)264 (35)	6)354 (36)

37 TWO AND THREE-DIGIT DIVISION

NAME: DATE: TIME: SCORE: /36

2)102	5)185	4)292	5)315	7)385	2)24
1	2	3	4	5	6
2)60	4)116	3)156	2)114	3)162	2)156
7	8	9	10	11	12
2)70	5)355	6)420	7)448	6)198	7)651
13	14	15	16	17	18
6)462	3)222	3)36	7)357	5)415	3)63
19	20	21	22	23	24
5)145	4)544	6)552	8)544	4)148	5)95
25	26	27	28	29	30
8)136	6)78	5)105	7)84	6)540	2)52
31	32	33	34	35	36

TWO AND THREE-DIGIT DIVISION

38

NAME:	DATE:	TIME:	SCORE: /36

1. 7)378	2. 8)120	3. 6)510	4. 2)20	5. 9)342	6. 5)60
7. 4)396	8. 8)144	9. 8)496	10. 8)112	11. 5)200	12. 2)156
13. 9)153	14. 8)464	15. 3)186	16. 2)122	17. 4)276	18. 8)392
19. 3)126	20. 8)184	21. 9)720	22. 5)105	23. 2)98	24. 7)273
25. 6)60	26. 4)76	27. 3)177	28. 3)39	29. 7)469	30. 5)430
31. 9)189	32. 3)162	33. 2)102	34. 6)276	35. 8)608	36. 3)228

39 TWO AND THREE-DIGIT DIVISION

NAME: DATE: TIME: SCORE: /36

4)196	3)231	2)102	6)96	8)520	9)846
1	2	3	4	5	6
9)288	3)159	4)192	2)22	9)126	3)237
7	8	9	10	11	12
8)312	5)440	5)155	2)154	9)531	5)495
13	14	15	16	17	18
6)324	7)287	9)783	8)760	3)162	7)448
19	20	21	22	23	24
8)752	3)171	9)495	3)66	7)609	6)564
25	26	27	28	29	30
8)672	7)224	9)756	7)679	3)48	5)365
31	32	33	34	35	36

TWO AND THREE-DIGIT DIVISION

40

NAME:	DATE:	TIME:	SCORE: /36

4)320	4)368	2)172	4)84	3)129	6)366
1	2	3	4	5	6
8)104	9)108	2)72	7)238	4)328	9)351
7	8	9	10	11	12
3)180	2)82	5)380	5)125	5)160	9)423
13	14	15	16	17	18
7)196	2)80	5)355	5)265	4)220	9)459
19	20	21	22	23	24
8)144	4)116	7)476	4)236	3)195	3)252
25	26	27	28	29	30
4)264	7)686	3)210	7)539	2)48	2)182
31	32	33	34	35	36

41 TWO AND THREE-DIGIT DIVISION

NAME: DATE: TIME: SCORE: /36

2)158	3)129	23)69	7)658	3)114	12)48
1	2	3	4	5	6
9)729	3)273	17)51	3)132	7)511	55)275
7	8	9	10	11	12
9)756	5)400	26)78	5)65	5)245	5)170
13	14	15	16	17	18
34)136	2)50	9)450	3)252	17)85	9)684
19	20	21	22	23	24
6)456	3)93	11)66	4)396	5)395	9)621
25	26	27	28	29	30
38)114	8)512	4)268	54)54	8)104	2)78
31	32	33	34	35	36

TWO AND THREE-DIGIT DIVISION

42

NAME:	DATE:	TIME:	SCORE: /36

2)34 1	3)297 2	34)136 3	8)208 4	6)222 5	26)130 6
2)124 7	9)756 8	46)92 9	8)144 10	7)728 11	55)440 12
6)396 13	5)445 14	79)79 15	7)280 16	6)294 17	9)531 18
24)168 19	5)285 20	4)364 21	5)205 22	15)45 23	7)196 24
6)228 25	3)204 26	16)112 27	6)162 28	4)184 29	3)150 30
57)114 31	8)728 32	2)192 33	84)168 34	3)51 35	6)372 36

43 TWO AND THREE-DIGIT DIVISION

NAME: DATE: TIME: SCORE: /36

8)584	8)792	43)43	8)320	4)228	66)132
1	2	3	4	5	6
2)62	9)108	85)340	2)150	4)312	16)112
7	8	9	10	11	12
7)406	5)230	11)55	7)357	9)396	7)287
13	14	15	16	17	18
30)210	7)434	5)410	9)747	36)252	9)585
19	20	21	22	23	24
5)135	6)228	29)174	3)261	4)68	2)32
25	26	27	28	29	30
80)240	4)284	6)150	29)174	4)280	2)94
31	32	33	34	35	36

TWO AND THREE-DIGIT DIVISION

44

NAME:	DATE:	TIME:	SCORE: /36

9)252	9)648	12)72	5)440	7)210	28)252
1	2	3	4	5	6
5)180	8)424	50)400	6)162	8)680	48)240
7	8	9	10	11	12
7)168	5)145	27)108	3)75	3)267	6)504
13	14	15	16	17	18
30)120	5)345	4)156	9)594	76)152	7)595
19	20	21	22	23	24
5)155	2)82	25)200	4)48	3)180	4)104
25	26	27	28	29	30
34)204	3)168	3)153	69)207	3)72	5)95
31	32	33	34	35	36

45

TWO AND THREE-DIGIT DIVISION

NAME: DATE: TIME: SCORE: /36

6)306 (1)	5)115 (2)	42)126 (3)	7)273 (4)	9)396 (5)	52)156 (6)
8)416 (7)	7)371 (8)	24)120 (9)	4)284 (10)	7)322 (11)	32)64 (12)
2)84 (13)	7)203 (14)	60)240 (15)	2)46 (16)	3)150 (17)	8)456 (18)
33)66 (19)	4)40 (20)	9)333 (21)	9)207 (22)	21)84 (23)	7)469 (24)
9)513 (25)	2)188 (26)	71)426 (27)	2)106 (28)	5)275 (29)	3)75 (30)
74)370 (31)	2)174 (32)	2)52 (33)	54)378 (34)	4)200 (35)	6)318 (36)

TWO AND THREE-DIGIT DIVISION

NAME: DATE: TIME: SCORE: /36

8)680 1	46)138 2	2)56 3	94)564 4	6)72 5	64)320 6
5)295 7	94)188 8	2)28 9	51)204 10	2)178 11	82)328 12
3)84 13	71)426 14	9)432 15	93)186 16	8)552 17	85)680 18
6)252 19	29)145 20	5)485 21	72)504 22	5)400 23	97)194 24
8)608 25	42)252 26	4)344 27	29)232 28	2)32 29	65)585 30
6)444 31	54)378 32	5)445 33	73)365 34	4)232 35	8)392 36

47 TWO AND THREE-DIGIT DIVISION

NAME: DATE: TIME: SCORE: /36

4)336 1	81)324 2	7)441 3	90)270 4	4)224 5	11)99 6
2)108 7	32)64 8	2)64 9	20)160 10	6)486 11	43)258 12
7)392 13	35)175 14	5)245 15	89)534 16	9)819 17	43)172 18
2)96 19	29)174 20	3)168 21	95)855 22	9)729 23	41)287 24
5)415 25	34)544 26	7)364 27	15)660 28	8)488 29	12)972 30
2)188 31	58)638 32	7)511 33	10)670 34	8)744 35	6)210 36

TWO AND THREE-DIGIT DIVISION

NAME:	DATE:	TIME:	SCORE: /36

8)488 (1)	15)465 (2)	5)255 (3)	13)299 (4)	2)194 (5)	20)380 (6)
4)316 (7)	12)216 (8)	6)192 (9)	50)550 (10)	7)623 (11)	18)864 (12)
8)352 (13)	23)575 (14)	9)216 (15)	18)864 (16)	4)164 (17)	19)950 (18)
4)144 (19)	15)900 (20)	5)225 (21)	27)513 (22)	3)234 (23)	43)731 (24)
9)360 (25)	15)945 (26)	2)100 (27)	17)629 (28)	8)80 (29)	11)132 (30)
9)504 (31)	19)798 (32)	6)408 (33)	24)336 (34)	2)120 (35)	6)318 (36)

49

TWO AND THREE-DIGIT DIVISION

NAME: DATE: TIME: SCORE: /36

3)81 1	14)546 2	7)280 3	60)960 4	5)50 5	42)798 6
9)747 7	21)546 8	3)39 9	66)858 10	6)264 11	15)555 12
7)490 13	24)456 14	5)80 15	19)190 16	8)680 17	11)638 18
2)120 19	11)528 20	3)234 21	45)900 22	2)178 23	49)931 24
2)134 25	39)468 26	2)158 27	12)936 28	2)100 29	26)806 30
8)480 31	22)858 32	7)448 33	32)928 34	6)156 35	6)228 36

TWO AND THREE-DIGIT DIVISION

50

NAME: DATE: TIME: SCORE: /36

$9\overline{)153}$ 1	$18\overline{)612}$ 2	$3\overline{)201}$ 3	$67\overline{)804}$ 4	$7\overline{)301}$ 5	$13\overline{)871}$ 6
$7\overline{)84}$ 7	$12\overline{)348}$ 8	$8\overline{)792}$ 9	$56\overline{)672}$ 10	$5\overline{)430}$ 11	$18\overline{)432}$ 12
$5\overline{)245}$ 13	$17\overline{)952}$ 14	$8\overline{)392}$ 15	$15\overline{)210}$ 16	$2\overline{)192}$ 17	$33\overline{)825}$ 18
$6\overline{)210}$ 19	$17\overline{)935}$ 20	$8\overline{)368}$ 21	$18\overline{)270}$ 22	$9\overline{)306}$ 23	$16\overline{)256}$ 24
$4\overline{)368}$ 25	$11\overline{)803}$ 26	$3\overline{)99}$ 27	$14\overline{)952}$ 28	$5\overline{)375}$ 29	$17\overline{)935}$ 30
$9\overline{)873}$ 31	$41\overline{)943}$ 32	$9\overline{)846}$ 33	$38\overline{)798}$ 34	$6\overline{)486}$ 35	$6\overline{)306}$ 36

MIXED MATH

NAME: DATE: TIME: SCORE: /42

1. 991 +498	2. 8)120	3. 8)912	4. 94 ×16	5. 2)334	6. 61 ×75
7. 3)120	8. 520 −199	9. 4)448	10. 77 ×92	11. 871 −546	12. 16 ×44
13. 3)810	14. 590 −364	15. 4)320	16. 667 +484	17. 988 −433	18. 8)584
19. 712 −279	20. 779 −761	21. 54 ×52	22. 920 +596	23. 85 ×19	24. 80 ×69
25. 926 +470	26. 861 −663	27. 874 −332	28. 876 +185	29. 496 −448	30. 732 −681
31. 140 +213	32. 42)798	33. 226 −119	34. 719 +747	35. 84 ×30	36. 266 +858
37. 404 +167	38. 704 +222	39. 33 ×66	40. 580 +170	41. 98 ×91	42. 3)585

MIXED MATH

52

NAME:	DATE:	TIME:	SCORE: /42

658 −328 (1)	6)486 (2)	6)672 (3)	648 +970 (4)	3)354 (5)	948 +606 (6)
9)675 (7)	464 +319 (8)	848 −210 (9)	2)472 (10)	971 −789 (11)	42 ×16 (12)
779 +105 (13)	22 ×14 (14)	854 −638 (15)	624 −360 (16)	495 +220 (17)	85 ×60 (18)
799 +763 (19)	53 ×79 (20)	65 ×32 (21)	825 +910 (22)	21)651 (23)	69 ×22 (24)
834 −545 (25)	625 +546 (26)	271 +649 (27)	883 −487 (28)	294 +469 (29)	5)200 (30)
62 ×52 (31)	860 −631 (32)	89 ×24 (33)	942 −196 (34)	4)648 (35)	298 −267 (36)
55 ×65 (37)	4)776 (38)	85 ×22 (39)	172 +465 (40)	5)675 (41)	930 −706 (42)

53

MIXED MATH

NAME: DATE: TIME: SCORE: /42

625 +161 1	3)618 2	91 ×57 3	86 ×10 4	43 ×50 5	768 +548 6
45 ×76 7	631 −389 8	58 ×76 9	903 +208 10	6)438 11	7)770 12
942 −496 13	8)544 14	381 +503 15	5)875 16	22 ×98 17	786 +351 18
8)608 19	64 ×13 20	590 −395 21	403 +122 22	8)128 23	707 +404 24
866 −306 25	755 −629 26	68 ×30 27	482 +324 28	57 ×88 29	7)189 30
993 −514 31	12)156 32	2)802 33	366 +712 34	621 −383 35	725 −579 36
8)456 37	191 +906 38	444 −404 39	13 ×43 40	870 −223 41	470 +103 42

MIXED MATH

54

NAME:	DATE:	TIME:	SCORE: /42

7)756 1	868 +864 2	7)749 3	63 ×34 4	7)602 5	676 −470 6
881 −806 7	52 ×31 8	253 +802 9	527 −317 10	9)405 11	719 −359 12
63 ×24 13	33 ×98 14	5)745 15	336 −290 16	447 +204 17	69 ×63 18
51 ×79 19	6)690 20	796 −225 21	919 −824 22	13 ×12 23	26 ×73 24
611 +556 25	282 +173 26	7)700 27	27 ×17 28	641 −446 29	74 ×43 30
353 −242 31	3)426 32	101 +418 33	531 −509 34	46 ×96 35	140 +758 36
802 +132 37	7)525 38	127 +892 39	250 +690 40	768 −688 41	13)793 42

MIXED MATH

NAME: DATE: TIME: SCORE: /42

65 ×69 (1)	38 ×76 (2)	4)352 (3)	314 +482 (4)	603 −151 (5)	651 +656 (6)
26 ×28 (7)	56 ×32 (8)	6)570 (9)	942 −896 (10)	661 −273 (11)	227 −114 (12)
87 ×42 (13)	117 +328 (14)	743 −251 (15)	228 +236 (16)	819 −285 (17)	6)612 (18)
6)684 (19)	769 −515 (20)	4)616 (21)	842 +372 (22)	282 −219 (23)	34 ×20 (24)
92 ×49 (25)	9)909 (26)	4)508 (27)	891 +359 (28)	95 ×49 (29)	732 +325 (30)
96 ×24 (31)	4)732 (32)	20 ×20 (33)	982 −102 (34)	516 −146 (35)	4)720 (36)
702 +145 (37)	86 ×88 (38)	3)606 (39)	491 +686 (40)	878 +377 (41)	12)456 (42)

MIXED MATH

56

NAME: DATE: TIME: SCORE: /42

$4\overline{)696}$ (1)	$6\overline{)726}$ (2)	863 + 520 (3)	583 + 175 (4)	70 × 53 (5)	982 − 621 (6)
733 + 288 (7)	$5\overline{)640}$ (8)	60 × 37 (9)	853 − 491 (10)	$2\overline{)838}$ (11)	78 × 72 (12)
$9\overline{)405}$ (13)	874 + 730 (14)	147 + 516 (15)	491 − 437 (16)	760 − 158 (17)	10 × 77 (18)
$14\overline{)602}$ (19)	719 + 349 (20)	841 + 261 (21)	65 × 31 (22)	677 − 276 (23)	30 × 38 (24)
925 − 652 (25)	308 + 998 (26)	63 × 69 (27)	14 × 71 (28)	$7\overline{)434}$ (29)	247 + 361 (30)
765 − 348 (31)	278 + 136 (32)	67 × 17 (33)	$5\overline{)315}$ (34)	26 × 66 (35)	924 − 560 (36)
83 × 19 (37)	523 − 137 (38)	$6\overline{)852}$ (39)	842 − 585 (40)	$7\overline{)882}$ (41)	$4\overline{)368}$ (42)

57

MIXED MATH

NAME: DATE: TIME: SCORE: /42

423 +979 (1)	19 ×88 (2)	345 +351 (3)	57 ×92 (4)	460 +159 (5)	860 −512 (6)
15 ×79 (7)	3)813 (8)	683 −267 (9)	9)486 (10)	965 −281 (11)	471 −197 (12)
24 ×38 (13)	585 +813 (14)	3)117 (15)	8)336 (16)	2)466 (17)	425 +791 (18)
562 −454 (19)	139 +183 (20)	974 +288 (21)	160 −114 (22)	17 ×62 (23)	750 +960 (24)
6)378 (25)	6)552 (26)	803 −216 (27)	24 ×33 (28)	83 ×94 (29)	30 ×31 (30)
4)328 (31)	22)308 (32)	74 ×90 (33)	93 ×82 (34)	782 +510 (35)	837 −626 (36)
265 −116 (37)	3)936 (38)	570 −107 (39)	771 +127 (40)	3)609 (41)	13 ×51 (42)

MIXED MATH

58

NAME: DATE: TIME: SCORE: /42

6)834 1	6)546 2	974 −655 3	965 −684 4	8)736 5	673 −164 6
13 ×59 7	785 −418 8	36 ×60 9	44 ×13 10	873 +106 11	876 −174 12
77 ×45 13	360 +239 14	6)156 15	882 −146 16	7)511 17	37 ×85 18
17 ×38 19	8)544 20	869 −118 21	8)824 22	973 −869 23	540 +419 24
7)420 25	727 +303 26	288 +828 27	354 −219 28	76 ×35 29	702 −429 30
47 ×62 31	8)160 32	30 ×62 33	948 +442 34	637 +149 35	990 +620 36
13 ×50 37	64 ×39 38	8)112 39	810 +711 40	16)640 41	611 +437 42

59

MIXED MATH

NAME: DATE: TIME: SCORE: /42

967 −354 1	51 ×37 2	40 ×93 3	14)630 4	494 +575 5	31 ×86 6
847 +870 7	2)744 8	570 +593 9	8)696 10	120 −110 11	4)512 12
968 −708 13	918 +668 14	85 ×27 15	6)198 16	425 +311 17	49 ×87 18
365 −310 19	721 +754 20	31 ×18 21	546 +270 22	4)920 23	9)477 24
978 +383 25	9)630 26	44 ×73 27	395 −260 28	586 −279 29	5)595 30
65 ×36 31	616 −213 32	69 ×43 33	8)392 34	555 −272 35	3)324 36
322 +578 37	598 +707 38	532 −185 39	49 ×74 40	845 −322 41	40 ×57 42

MIXED MATH

60

NAME: DATE: TIME: SCORE: /42

(1) 692 +369	(2) 651 −306	(3) 2)626	(4) 5)325	(5) 852 +399	(6) 91 ×67
(7) 6)594	(8) 19 ×52	(9) 8)576	(10) 16 ×67	(11) 5)610	(12) 853 −474
(13) 96 ×20	(14) 570 −498	(15) 53 ×23	(16) 73 ×61	(17) 912 −118	(18) 693 +817
(19) 985 +246	(20) 34)748	(21) 790 −591	(22) 996 +722	(23) 354 +165	(24) 566 −213
(25) 724 +269	(26) 943 −605	(27) 960 −829	(28) 20 ×54	(29) 272 +589	(30) 7)343
(31) 466 −151	(32) 18 ×66	(33) 361 +430	(34) 57 ×61	(35) 38 ×76	(36) 5)380
(37) 443 +994	(38) 18 ×37	(39) 6)534	(40) 8)248	(41) 7)686	(42) 629 −222

61 MIXED MATH

NAME: DATE: TIME: SCORE: /42

747 −110 1	363 −257 2	104 +223 3	8)472 4	39 ×98 5	3)345 6
854 +745 7	580 −308 8	13 ×38 9	15 ×90 10	55 ×84 11	42 ×14 12
862 −267 13	29 ×71 14	30 ×45 15	8)336 16	49 ×60 17	4)108 18
844 −315 19	9)819 20	709 +581 21	20 ×38 22	435 +553 23	41 ×87 24
828 −286 25	9)297 26	442 −174 27	7)245 28	4)256 29	781 +952 30
8)744 31	403 +178 32	903 +888 33	2)312 34	710 +368 35	481 +124 36
811 +290 37	347 −309 38	22)902 39	710 −583 40	86 ×67 41	715 −419 42

MIXED MATH

62

NAME: DATE: TIME: SCORE: /42

267 −167 1	9)522 2	3)519 3	942 −147 4	8)808 5	183 +983 6
202 +226 7	623 +977 8	842 −484 9	381 +389 10	87 ×52 11	957 +869 12
17 ×53 13	150 +365 14	869 −623 15	8)912 16	132 +238 17	892 −576 18
8)392 19	8)488 20	37)740 21	40 ×49 22	989 −646 23	842 −311 24
93 ×74 25	844 −611 26	8)416 27	70 ×11 28	55 ×42 29	5)535 30
446 +909 31	35 ×20 32	510 +838 33	27 ×46 34	358 −188 35	981 +846 36
2)484 37	8)384 38	71 ×31 39	45 ×37 40	848 −344 41	66 ×84 42

63 MIXED MATH

NAME: DATE: TIME: SCORE: /42

73 ×95 1	9)846 2	824 +291 3	780 –369 4	5)860 5	539 +297 6
65 ×54 7	17 ×76 8	8)760 9	57 ×57 10	12 ×59 11	2)766 12
486 –430 13	381 +595 14	178 –155 15	73 ×17 16	814 +726 17	380 +923 18
3)777 19	272 +247 20	6)210 21	833 +293 22	174 +215 23	14)630 24
676 +506 25	7)539 26	8)952 27	829 –157 28	68 ×89 29	8)160 30
779 –773 31	66 ×85 32	266 –240 33	550 +646 34	93 ×64 35	830 –493 36
751 –345 37	23 ×20 38	895 –669 39	2)934 40	60 ×22 41	992 –902 42

MIXED MATH

64

NAME:	DATE:	TIME:	SCORE: /42

689 −152 (1)	79 ×79 (2)	9)936 (3)	5)430 (4)	794 −255 (5)	9)666 (6)
20 ×87 (7)	5)190 (8)	832 −150 (9)	61 ×61 (10)	244 +260 (11)	496 +563 (12)
616 −433 (13)	920 +434 (14)	48 ×16 (15)	947 +961 (16)	87 ×86 (17)	23 ×21 (18)
9)387 (19)	129 +517 (20)	2)766 (21)	19 ×73 (22)	612 −312 (23)	774 −423 (24)
73 ×35 (25)	16)640 (26)	406 +538 (27)	9)756 (28)	10 ×15 (29)	975 +919 (30)
8)136 (31)	848 −243 (32)	656 +766 (33)	847 −318 (34)	4)236 (35)	326 +341 (36)
94 ×13 (37)	306 +669 (38)	870 −741 (39)	3)246 (40)	45 ×33 (41)	953 −149 (42)

MIXED MATH

NAME: DATE: TIME: SCORE: /42

1: 5)180	2: 70 ×68	3: 257 +785	4: 794 −672	5: 404 +749	6: 388 −159
7: 7)763	8: 763 +802	9: 353 −143	10: 146 +694	11: 63 ×18	12: 7)728
13: 547 −328	14: 78 ×21	15: 988 −796	16: 9)927	17: 104 +899	18: 421 +639
19: 706 −143	20: 71 ×20	21: 73 ×96	22: 22)308	23: 84 ×72	24: 49 ×71
25: 212 +461	26: 930 −821	27: 348 −233	28: 733 −146	29: 50 ×47	30: 2)150
31: 566 −354	32: 76 ×65	33: 183 +916	34: 2)690	35: 9)252	36: 6)600
37: 7)420	38: 38 ×31	39: 389 +488	40: 10 ×40	41: 470 +457	42: 9)342

MIXED MATH

66

NAME:	DATE:	TIME:	SCORE: /42

$9\overline{)801}$ 1	$396 - 192$ 2	32×82 3	$134 + 660$ 4	$3\overline{)429}$ 5	$917 + 888$ 6
$880 - 369$ 7	$944 - 151$ 8	$9\overline{)369}$ 9	$8\overline{)784}$ 10	$209 + 105$ 11	60×38 12
$4\overline{)320}$ 13	$203 + 578$ 14	44×52 15	$215 + 502$ 16	$372 + 153$ 17	$312 - 265$ 18
$706 + 643$ 19	$5\overline{)275}$ 20	79×65 21	$981 - 161$ 22	$819 + 319$ 23	$355 - 312$ 24
$7\overline{)161}$ 25	43×67 26	$6\overline{)786}$ 27	$988 - 359$ 28	96×88 29	$5\overline{)615}$ 30
$865 - 306$ 31	$679 - 173$ 32	45×42 33	96×62 34	$582 + 364$ 35	$916 + 541$ 36
40×44 37	14×89 38	$8\overline{)336}$ 39	63×47 40	$12\overline{)984}$ 41	$614 - 200$ 42

67 MIXED MATH

NAME: DATE: TIME: SCORE: /42

52 ×17 1	329 +322 2	164 +598 3	86 ×87 4	95 ×24 5	504 –219 6
8)432 7	109 +927 8	877 –199 9	95 ×27 10	7)868 11	569 +301 12
91 ×90 13	35 ×65 14	16)864 15	609 –306 16	549 –189 17	862 –769 18
6)954 19	4)352 20	841 –728 21	12 ×91 22	726 –462 23	903 –139 24
663 +965 25	739 –362 26	976 +814 27	5)515 28	751 –332 29	7)707 30
74 ×35 31	975 +947 32	569 +226 33	8)600 34	3)726 35	92 ×54 36
753 +989 37	15 ×13 38	24 ×70 39	163 +507 40	5)440 41	7)497 42

MIXED MATH

68

NAME: DATE: TIME: SCORE: /42

61 ×51 1	6)510 2	251 +152 3	83 ×71 4	23 ×78 5	617 +432 6
344 −166 7	606 −111 8	2)934 9	575 −112 10	692 −124 11	628 +476 12
58 ×83 13	4)584 14	45 ×26 15	44 ×47 16	749 +752 17	76 ×94 18
328 +777 19	714 +706 20	3)234 21	8)256 22	9)504 23	49 ×79 24
905 −459 25	940 −663 26	892 +938 27	6)600 28	603 +607 29	848 −359 30
33)891 31	98 ×96 32	986 −590 33	6)744 34	952 −628 35	2)860 36
2)202 37	509 −245 38	43 ×55 39	85 ×74 40	764 +911 41	159 +157 42

69 MIXED MATH

NAME: DATE: TIME: SCORE: /42

930 −136 1	737 −207 2	47 ×78 3	605 +685 4	992 −423 5	6)342 6
9)468 7	383 −291 8	92 ×94 9	388 +507 10	384 −173 11	339 −219 12
40 ×82 13	9)747 14	9)702 15	434 +722 16	6)240 17	59 ×18 18
703 +595 19	5)475 20	887 −634 21	579 +468 22	901 −615 23	84 ×35 24
761 +903 25	90 ×31 26	968 +102 27	845 +432 28	4)796 29	33 ×48 30
73 ×41 31	5)875 32	24)360 33	32 ×80 34	815 −133 35	7)826 36
900 +422 37	798 +141 38	7)476 39	60 ×76 40	26 ×58 41	632 −629 42

MIXED MATH

70

NAME: DATE: TIME: SCORE: /42

3)591 1	594 +745 2	9)693 3	971 −622 4	4)412 5	640 −223 6
951 −506 7	771 +305 8	41 ×73 9	186 +289 10	789 −680 11	934 −288 12
944 +453 13	871 +831 14	58 ×83 15	74 ×50 16	448 +357 17	446 −437 18
606 −270 19	868 −325 20	24 ×40 21	772 −738 22	12 ×55 23	13)325 24
9)414 25	9)612 26	451 +662 27	8)712 28	20 ×25 29	9)117 30
3)846 31	59 ×58 32	4)812 33	838 +296 34	869 +554 35	16 ×65 36
84 ×65 37	891 +424 38	96 ×25 39	7)217 40	33 ×35 41	903 −110 42

MIXED MATH

NAME: DATE: TIME: SCORE: /42

46 ×96 1	6)102 2	34 ×47 3	4)868 4	241 +197 5	40 ×42 6
44 ×17 7	529 +811 8	6)510 9	3)576 10	80 ×65 11	858 −321 12
13 ×80 13	971 +559 14	886 −160 15	234 +881 16	52 ×12 17	20 ×71 18
672 −218 19	582 −213 20	4)732 21	2)660 22	862 −116 23	4)100 24
22 ×90 25	520 +950 26	750 +454 27	6)408 28	399 −376 29	16)640 30
60 ×13 31	584 +262 32	991 −958 33	202 +714 34	819 −261 35	767 −359 36
368 +680 37	2)126 38	299 +692 39	714 −396 40	9)675 41	37 ×83 42

MIXED MATH

NAME: DATE: TIME: SCORE: /42

2)958 1	286 +885 2	460 −440 3	888 −230 4	4)476 5	26 ×75 6
5)895 7	980 −222 8	61 ×66 9	43 ×17 10	531 +548 11	630 −318 12
22 ×92 13	642 −401 14	308 +243 15	9)585 16	70 ×38 17	774 −317 18
27 ×80 19	460 −170 20	711 −289 21	948 +879 22	4)840 23	718 +762 24
976 −770 25	783 +696 26	48 ×57 27	9)846 28	447 −409 29	4)492 30
29)522 31	489 +724 32	7)763 33	183 +565 34	17 ×48 35	31 ×17 36
5)505 37	33 ×15 38	980 +216 39	44 ×89 40	781 +233 41	8)776 42

73 MIXED MATH

NAME: DATE: TIME: SCORE: /42

552 +537 1	9)495 2	992 −265 3	7)203 4	2)916 5	230 +429 6
932 +990 7	10 ×34 8	393 −222 9	2)258 10	63 ×47 11	507 −499 12
6)846 13	6)198 14	791 +644 15	7)567 16	578 −435 17	64 ×81 18
71 ×59 19	43 ×17 20	798 −293 21	705 +332 22	2)662 23	986 −364 24
105 +447 25	71 ×79 26	129 +705 27	56)840 28	14 ×88 29	41 ×93 30
837 −349 31	875 +398 32	33 ×37 33	503 −437 34	29 ×50 35	5)305 36
959 −900 37	68 ×87 38	815 +798 39	433 +235 40	858 −725 41	9)324 42

MIXED MATH

74

NAME: DATE: TIME: SCORE: /42

7)532 1	930 +900 2	64 ×12 3	779 −699 4	7)301 5	96 ×28 6
50 ×62 7	17)765 8	958 −129 9	949 −710 10	947 +665 11	5)610 12
163 +194 13	8)120 14	8)296 15	295 +725 16	805 −617 17	5)260 18
82 ×97 19	710 −141 20	109 +376 21	279 +889 22	2)300 23	32 ×65 24
31 ×83 25	53 ×56 26	8)240 27	70 ×38 28	217 −117 29	825 +204 30
998 −229 31	415 +936 32	3)501 33	705 +146 34	520 −414 35	77 ×79 36
892 −347 37	31 ×33 38	881 −544 39	9)369 40	60 ×73 41	136 +973 42

75

MIXED MATH

NAME: DATE: TIME: SCORE: /42

271 +971 1	797 −254 2	775 +942 3	812 −465 4	6)774 5	936 +367 6
720 +171 7	191 +229 8	5)395 9	51 ×34 10	856 +202 11	2)774 12
61 ×17 13	844 −135 14	64 ×13 15	58 ×90 16	18)648 17	990 −369 18
521 −519 19	890 −716 20	935 −671 21	9)954 22	9)153 23	60 ×48 24
878 +294 25	156 +671 26	78 ×29 27	49 ×86 28	35 ×71 29	4)604 30
525 +283 31	579 −291 32	936 −245 33	69 ×23 34	6)882 35	65 ×18 36
327 +993 37	5)760 38	4)124 39	88 ×24 40	344 −172 41	7)441 42

MIXED MATH

76

NAME:	DATE:	TIME:	SCORE: /42

52 ×12 (1)	216 −122 (2)	655 +884 (3)	31)558 (4)	658 −473 (5)	2)178 (6)
655 +311 (7)	210 +244 (8)	86 ×31 (9)	6)420 (10)	6)798 (11)	42 ×92 (12)
4)556 (13)	30 ×31 (14)	709 −494 (15)	37 ×11 (16)	549 −232 (17)	565 +133 (18)
3)315 (19)	697 −594 (20)	601 +532 (21)	737 +700 (22)	52 ×38 (23)	422 +354 (24)
91 ×37 (25)	88 ×52 (26)	798 −433 (27)	79 ×11 (28)	7)350 (29)	933 −161 (30)
6)168 (31)	33 ×28 (32)	240 +349 (33)	435 −277 (34)	46 ×71 (35)	787 −214 (36)
6)558 (37)	2)496 (38)	2)244 (39)	280 +861 (40)	212 +668 (41)	651 −182 (42)

77 MIXED MATH

NAME:	DATE:	TIME:	SCORE: /42

816 −650 1	829 +833 2	748 −459 3	7)273 4	687 −316 5	3)429 6
2)810 7	666 −411 8	79 ×44 9	816 +521 10	24)528 11	981 −604 12
709 −131 13	21 ×87 14	5)840 15	102 +310 16	900 −144 17	20 ×54 18
8)320 19	39 ×24 20	67 ×52 21	78 ×31 22	686 +824 23	238 +425 24
3)117 25	643 −279 26	8)832 27	772 −378 28	842 +262 29	7)966 30
83 ×19 31	242 +336 32	58 ×87 33	75 ×67 34	656 +189 35	7)945 36
889 −854 37	271 +763 38	693 +684 39	98 ×28 40	9)351 41	54 ×95 42

MIXED MATH

78

NAME: DATE: TIME: SCORE: /42

51 ×83 1	71 ×53 2	2)316 3	92 ×83 4	568 −299 5	953 +878 6
650 −608 7	47 ×64 8	689 −445 9	888 −223 10	996 −833 11	8)208 12
7)945 13	37 ×51 14	8)440 15	476 +484 16	93 ×24 17	751 +254 18
5)980 19	54 ×11 20	9)234 21	4)736 22	186 −120 23	50 ×79 24
363 +587 25	83 ×76 26	4)112 27	867 −666 28	885 −552 29	49 ×60 30
891 +814 31	9)846 32	7)112 33	815 −471 34	137 +219 35	506 +875 36
635 +299 37	84 ×10 38	791 +262 39	310 +818 40	873 −659 41	15)945 42

MIXED MATH

NAME: DATE: TIME: SCORE: /42

1. 4)796	2. 856 −352	3. 19 ×68	4. 741 −530	5. 6)174	6. 34 ×79
7. 9)270	8. 4)368	9. 437 +444	10. 68 ×57	11. 3)108	12. 189 +783
13. 601 −113	14. 800 −297	15. 21 ×31	16. 920 −168	17. 998 −744	18. 8)656
19. 602 −186	20. 174 +573	21. 807 +657	22. 62 ×48	23. 13 ×84	24. 8)848
25. 699 +428	26. 50 ×32	27. 864 −396	28. 63 ×27	29. 96 ×44	30. 94 ×24
31. 816 +889	32. 982 −285	33. 228 +925	34. 16)512	35. 683 +813	36. 3)414
37. 62 ×17	38. 962 −266	39. 6)432	40. 850 +947	41. 2)934	42. 671 +690

MIXED MATH

80

NAME: DATE: TIME: SCORE: /42

792 −568 1	32 ×45 2	5)420 3	775 +322 4	908 +844 5	551 −425 6
6)684 7	79 ×15 8	19)779 9	319 +781 10	840 −566 11	140 +733 12
34 ×85 13	2)358 14	29 ×47 15	503 −347 16	8)904 17	56 ×67 18
487 +881 19	7)686 20	200 +391 21	33 ×30 22	951 +364 23	859 −167 24
77 ×75 25	566 −361 26	9)558 27	443 +366 28	916 −328 29	48 ×14 30
3)600 31	809 −609 32	731 +897 33	2)778 34	318 −256 35	98 ×50 36
36 ×78 37	61 ×90 38	4)664 39	947 −314 40	2)714 41	682 +131 42

81

MIXED MATH

NAME: DATE: TIME: SCORE: /42

22)242 1	891 −630 2	96 ×54 3	786 +626 4	357 +842 5	63 ×28 6
27 ×69 7	616 −204 8	849 +530 9	864 −574 10	434 +419 11	173 +294 12
79 ×40 13	664 +197 14	6)306 15	15 ×66 16	7)210 17	651 −381 18
2)122 19	29 ×59 20	6)876 21	367 +763 22	792 −671 23	940 −349 24
445 +462 25	695 −437 26	2)554 27	8)520 28	704 +125 29	7)364 30
66 ×71 31	47 ×93 32	5)410 33	22 ×84 34	5)595 35	7)511 36
358 −203 37	39 ×96 38	134 +868 39	685 −397 40	70 ×84 41	582 −551 42

MIXED MATH

82

NAME:	DATE:	TIME:	SCORE: /42

705 −392 1	7)259 2	938 −446 3	22 ×28 4	537 +212 5	654 +760 6
904 +899 7	786 +114 8	435 −269 9	407 +477 10	87 ×74 11	6)654 12
524 +747 13	96 ×22 14	109 +145 15	557 +911 16	74 ×30 17	13 ×81 18
9)657 19	659 −233 20	345 −267 21	709 +152 22	2)876 23	207 −168 24
5)600 25	51 ×28 26	2)820 27	8)768 28	21)609 29	2)436 30
32 ×18 31	241 −206 32	38 ×58 33	21 ×86 34	8)664 35	433 +424 36
30 ×66 37	8)280 38	320 −178 39	45 ×26 40	526 −509 41	768 −427 42

83

MIXED MATH

NAME: DATE: TIME: SCORE: /42

631 −100 1	992 +647 2	947 −314 3	968 +819 4	67 ×71 5	185 +811 6
78 ×33 7	287 +934 8	30 ×71 9	2)756 10	851 −595 11	9)108 12
747 +331 13	506 −330 14	828 −261 15	994 +587 16	48 ×46 17	856 +326 18
3)939 19	9)972 20	12 ×42 21	582 +361 22	58 ×43 23	20 ×57 24
5)350 25	958 −691 26	47)893 27	682 +615 28	6)558 29	611 −360 30
360 −202 31	5)890 32	26 ×36 33	836 −160 34	70 ×72 35	14 ×42 36
9)558 37	69 ×98 38	5)230 39	670 +181 40	9)360 41	821 −820 42

MIXED MATH

84

NAME: DATE: TIME: SCORE: /42

9)585 1	607 +318 2	373 −184 3	587 −468 4	2)674 5	226 +947 6
862 −634 7	278 +201 8	4)768 9	9)351 10	29 ×71 11	90 ×17 12
728 −573 13	231 +238 14	7)672 15	90 ×27 16	722 +992 17	755 −234 18
9)738 19	43 ×38 20	2)600 21	764 −374 22	81 ×69 23	41 ×52 24
895 −158 25	7)917 26	30 ×85 27	115 +338 28	13 ×24 29	64 ×98 30
135 +933 31	814 −398 32	413 −341 33	18)738 34	55 ×10 35	587 −473 36
6)654 37	5)775 38	984 +543 39	91 ×96 40	873 +730 41	376 +260 42

85 MIXED MATH

NAME:	DATE:	TIME:	SCORE: /42

558 −427 1	6)282 2	360 +665 3	7)847 4	92 ×21 5	2)184 6
2)410 7	695 −613 8	942 −442 9	22 ×67 10	83)996 11	84 ×49 12
45 ×54 13	49 ×58 14	816 −174 15	68 ×47 16	672 +764 17	844 −626 18
965 +475 19	321 +171 20	712 +988 21	71 ×12 22	73 ×72 23	143 +765 24
33 ×97 25	17 ×39 26	4)596 27	2)868 28	327 +522 29	147 −101 30
899 −186 31	673 −533 32	3)312 33	8)280 34	812 −536 35	633 −328 36
3)267 37	185 +162 38	4)160 39	34 ×75 40	531 +431 41	981 +741 42

MIXED MATH

86

NAME:	DATE:	TIME:	SCORE: /42

28 ×19 1	389 −250 2	584 −353 3	6)942 4	780 +852 5	2)966 6
7)665 7	690 −573 8	56 ×66 9	23)529 10	8)416 11	667 −169 12
98 ×28 13	9)639 14	3)135 15	73 ×87 16	161 +519 17	669 −405 18
937 −231 19	540 +343 20	6)918 21	67 ×90 22	2)884 23	6)126 24
817 +404 25	51 ×45 26	826 −382 27	965 +913 28	528 −163 29	6)162 30
90 ×31 31	221 +310 32	40 ×11 33	971 −868 34	35 ×22 35	898 +211 36
10 ×10 37	332 +771 38	13 ×84 39	315 +468 40	929 −382 41	559 +262 42

87 MIXED MATH

NAME: DATE: TIME: SCORE: /42

4)880 1	362 +301 2	540 +271 3	4)596 4	981 −777 5	5)290 6
92 ×56 7	38 ×87 8	946 +385 9	6)744 10	771 −494 11	51 ×20 12
856 +188 13	61 ×61 14	681 −573 15	291 +359 16	7)693 17	116 +630 18
251 +468 19	65 ×19 20	691 +599 21	62 ×72 22	74 ×49 23	761 +876 24
5)215 25	5)450 26	61 ×12 27	26)598 28	465 −141 29	921 +646 30
62 ×46 31	390 −346 32	87 ×10 33	5)605 34	985 −888 35	3)582 36
545 −288 37	753 −339 38	98 ×27 39	350 −111 40	6)582 41	450 −235 42

MIXED MATH

88

NAME:	DATE:	TIME:	SCORE: /42

785 +204 1	8)536 2	63 ×77 3	869 −477 4	48 ×84 5	5)815 6
8)472 7	22 ×78 8	523 +494 9	620 −280 10	898 +377 11	721 +490 12
917 +345 13	2)524 14	96 ×77 15	6)288 16	39 ×12 17	686 +786 18
801 +473 19	569 −258 20	929 −511 21	13)286 22	6)666 23	941 +354 24
3)900 25	121 +916 26	8)768 27	910 −881 28	66 ×29 29	871 −418 30
73 ×90 31	70 ×11 32	201 −176 33	119 +133 34	29 ×56 35	420 −117 36
614 −164 37	28 ×20 38	866 −753 39	6)738 40	86 ×75 41	5)875 42

89

MIXED MATH

NAME: DATE: TIME: SCORE: /42

883 −167 (1)	769 −445 (2)	607 −271 (3)	135 +356 (4)	385 +579 (5)	27 ×36 (6)
76 ×83 (7)	915 +933 (8)	5)555 (9)	9)540 (10)	275 +432 (11)	576 +692 (12)
8)704 (13)	15)615 (14)	848 −546 (15)	36 ×75 (16)	84 ×77 (17)	2)420 (18)
9)918 (19)	5)750 (20)	174 +472 (21)	55 ×43 (22)	526 −117 (23)	84 ×79 (24)
180 +344 (25)	93 ×41 (26)	66 ×16 (27)	2)106 (28)	627 −624 (29)	48 ×62 (30)
2)918 (31)	557 +156 (32)	20 ×57 (33)	44 ×23 (34)	6)660 (35)	970 −960 (36)
750 +166 (37)	329 −310 (38)	785 −606 (39)	783 +887 (40)	2)698 (41)	866 −568 (42)

MIXED MATH

NAME: DATE: TIME: SCORE: /42

1. 58 ×93	2. 4)620	3. 916 −379	4. 751 −727	5. 22 ×59	6. 19)285
7. 913 −380	8. 3)771	9. 15 ×29	10. 333 +188	11. 32 ×82	12. 50 ×40
13. 5)605	14. 74 ×33	15. 93 ×63	16. 6)834	17. 393 +230	18. 754 −339
19. 7)112	20. 222 +676	21. 30 ×88	22. 808 +150	23. 911 −675	24. 842 −369
25. 7)658	26. 452 +890	27. 556 −539	28. 88 ×63	29. 429 +912	30. 55 ×79
31. 7)924	32. 953 +242	33. 8)312	34. 558 +277	35. 13 ×15	36. 670 −476
37. 688 +497	38. 9)801	39. 800 +295	40. 4)212	41. 629 −165	42. 358 −175

91 MIXED MATH

NAME: DATE: TIME: SCORE: /42

221 +387 1	5)435 2	989 −197 3	7)735 4	20 ×88 5	849 +114 6
11)506 7	26 ×39 8	317 −122 9	376 +774 10	6)810 11	21 ×74 12
7)175 13	662 −550 14	97 ×67 15	444 +850 16	59 ×80 17	6)762 18
983 −313 19	754 −332 20	355 −187 21	9)666 22	50 ×69 23	753 −274 24
9)405 25	94 ×39 26	430 −312 27	7)567 28	186 +282 29	5)370 30
79 ×86 31	203 −147 32	817 −519 33	335 +155 34	368 +241 35	72 ×38 36
2)204 37	89 ×57 38	443 +581 39	73 ×43 40	492 +354 41	288 +423 42

MIXED MATH

92

NAME:	DATE:	TIME:	SCORE: /42

4)228 (1)	675 −358 (2)	5)855 (3)	93 ×45 (4)	33)495 (5)	33 ×32 (6)
9)171 (7)	854 −404 (8)	41 ×91 (9)	882 −176 (10)	78 ×68 (11)	5)820 (12)
47 ×69 (13)	772 +867 (14)	430 +692 (15)	78 ×67 (16)	3)285 (17)	17 ×26 (18)
41 ×18 (19)	109 +146 (20)	81 ×51 (21)	9)702 (22)	825 −783 (23)	552 −153 (24)
171 +603 (25)	381 +604 (26)	9)747 (27)	5)235 (28)	6)534 (29)	588 −374 (30)
837 +313 (31)	423 +747 (32)	802 +108 (33)	23 ×74 (34)	273 +570 (35)	452 −220 (36)
6)258 (37)	70 ×80 (38)	463 −230 (39)	796 +167 (40)	928 −614 (41)	851 −385 (42)

93 MIXED MATH

NAME: DATE: TIME: SCORE: /42

945 −416 1	68 ×35 2	498 −457 3	162 +257 4	737 +536 5	71 ×51 6
33 ×10 7	8)944 8	95 ×79 9	117 +941 10	2)586 11	11)935 12
100 +464 13	280 +929 14	3)465 15	638 −522 16	10 ×73 17	7)560 18
9)729 19	43 ×73 20	961 −583 21	7)350 22	9)567 23	23 ×80 24
4)376 25	815 +468 26	552 +925 27	57 ×34 28	516 +554 29	57 ×19 30
74 ×71 31	348 −313 32	563 +520 33	985 −345 34	636 −587 35	3)579 36
545 −101 37	5)895 38	360 +606 39	75 ×17 40	631 −465 41	809 −640 42

MIXED MATH

NAME: DATE: TIME: SCORE: /42

219 +907 (1)	384 −147 (2)	682 −542 (3)	22 ×60 (4)	6)648 (5)	7)336 (6)
76 ×39 (7)	9)666 (8)	47 ×52 (9)	37)555 (10)	349 +414 (11)	24 ×74 (12)
502 +780 (13)	22 ×62 (14)	587 −103 (15)	617 +183 (16)	3)966 (17)	62 ×22 (18)
5)635 (19)	85 ×14 (20)	835 −593 (21)	7)609 (22)	44 ×23 (23)	186 +799 (24)
276 −234 (25)	10 ×32 (26)	317 +237 (27)	399 +944 (28)	36 ×43 (29)	701 −410 (30)
715 −123 (31)	7)511 (32)	735 +599 (33)	83 ×28 (34)	3)876 (35)	639 −544 (36)
3)384 (37)	319 −231 (38)	860 +511 (39)	986 +802 (40)	6)924 (41)	714 −708 (42)

95 MIXED MATH

NAME: DATE: TIME: SCORE: /42

$2\overline{)918}$ 1	24 ×71 2	36 ×93 3	$3\overline{)102}$ 4	68 ×15 5	$7\overline{)588}$ 6
12 ×43 7	898 −780 8	102 +856 9	177 +394 10	$9\overline{)963}$ 11	12 ×25 12
399 +112 13	$2\overline{)118}$ 14	962 −655 15	388 +920 16	911 −249 17	$6\overline{)882}$ 18
$2\overline{)152}$ 19	$8\overline{)784}$ 20	720 −258 21	733 −548 22	997 +297 23	828 −617 24
46 ×11 25	54 ×80 26	$18\overline{)900}$ 27	494 +733 28	714 −231 29	895 +598 30
593 +696 31	203 +825 32	$9\overline{)306}$ 33	567 +341 34	20 ×68 35	408 −295 36
607 −506 37	$3\overline{)354}$ 38	59 ×88 39	15 ×28 40	764 −733 41	49 ×59 42

MIXED MATH

96

NAME:	DATE:	TIME:	SCORE: /42

23 ×40 (1)	629 +985 (2)	796 −349 (3)	16 ×50 (4)	551 −107 (5)	617 −341 (6)
62 ×34 (7)	22 ×29 (8)	2)372 (9)	45 ×28 (10)	897 +726 (11)	2)648 (12)
857 +873 (13)	80 ×18 (14)	3)555 (15)	723 −316 (16)	711 −668 (17)	25 ×57 (18)
54)702 (19)	9)612 (20)	694 −420 (21)	457 +365 (22)	938 +741 (23)	41 ×42 (24)
915 −510 (25)	6)258 (26)	921 −178 (27)	670 −474 (28)	6)894 (29)	13 ×48 (30)
6)162 (31)	509 +751 (32)	52 ×59 (33)	169 +987 (34)	9)207 (35)	674 +114 (36)
87 ×43 (37)	810 +207 (38)	588 −273 (39)	415 +481 (40)	2)236 (41)	5)930 (42)

97 MIXED MATH

NAME: DATE: TIME: SCORE: /42

82 ×87 1	3)153 2	815 −470 3	23 ×36 4	9)756 5	757 −393 6
14 ×19 7	950 −321 8	880 +976 9	982 +602 10	28 ×42 11	792 −785 12
38)570 13	4)856 14	81 ×69 15	71 ×12 16	257 −167 17	283 +849 18
433 +262 19	456 −353 20	11 ×86 21	154 −103 22	38 ×56 23	86 ×75 24
368 +176 25	106 +872 26	8)856 27	524 +809 28	7)868 29	9)684 30
848 +372 31	945 −306 32	338 −250 33	6)744 34	25 ×34 35	803 +453 36
8)104 37	804 +258 38	51 ×51 39	666 −278 40	5)660 41	7)273 42

MIXED MATH

98

NAME: DATE: TIME: SCORE: /42

692 +680 1	879 +810 2	8)824 3	709 +914 4	787 +984 5	6)648 6
231 +918 7	18 ×27 8	57 ×60 9	51)816 10	42 ×20 11	62 ×16 12
392 –335 13	104 +515 14	288 –254 15	2)338 16	5)130 17	463 –441 18
49 ×51 19	8)392 20	165 +240 21	162 –128 22	34 ×91 23	75 ×49 24
22 ×56 25	526 –487 26	4)648 27	736 –656 28	569 –120 29	249 –112 30
231 +540 31	6)978 32	114 +359 33	952 –712 34	49 ×73 35	2)872 36
4)576 37	815 +770 38	214 –146 39	2)248 40	29 ×92 41	62 ×54 42

99

MIXED MATH

NAME: DATE: TIME: SCORE: /42

17 ×67 1	3)963 2	608 –577 3	525 –246 4	549 +820 5	148 –125 6
5)485 7	6)480 8	222 +969 9	3)348 10	963 +855 11	37 ×95 12
57 ×38 13	896 +899 14	844 –763 15	15)465 16	615 –489 17	7)812 18
75 ×92 19	6)138 20	947 +594 21	339 +463 22	15 ×11 23	409 –244 24
70 ×14 25	58 ×62 26	84 ×48 27	349 +686 28	18 ×50 29	524 +897 30
31 ×50 31	5)420 32	824 –569 33	715 –643 34	5)490 35	641 +601 36
214 +916 37	911 –728 38	8)760 39	729 –566 40	46 ×75 41	8)408 42

MIXED MATH

100

NAME: DATE: TIME: SCORE: /42

152 +109 1	526 +539 2	9)783 3	245 +847 4	812 +552 5	11)583 6
2)362 7	5)975 8	2)110 9	62 ×85 10	27 ×73 11	75 ×44 12
851 −218 13	686 −156 14	757 −251 15	8)896 16	7)798 17	40 ×53 18
72 ×50 19	649 −533 20	4)416 21	568 −213 22	68 ×18 23	21 ×90 24
656 +761 25	266 −196 26	39 ×78 27	762 −104 28	326 +219 29	417 −191 30
6)762 31	929 +872 32	2)146 33	516 +799 34	6)600 35	19 ×96 36
24 ×94 37	986 −350 38	623 +826 39	220 +545 40	82 ×47 41	701 −421 42

ANSWERS

	1	2	3	4	5	6	7
1.	224	308	440	170	304	981	6345
2.	387	155	702	0	45	1792	3124
3.	87	21	351	17	532	1024	3472
4.	224	325	76	194	86	4295	2274
5.	104	100	448	434	180	511	1285
6.	308	462	138	148	161	4764	4655
7.	380	0	93	378	165	2925	0
8.	126	200	305	110	594	4401	920
9.	126	198	704	260	256	7592	5154
10.	264	273	0	288	67	2406	0
11.	20	162	0	0	80	0	4527
12.	336	112	68	711	53	1545	4864
13.	128	528	486	210	189	1290	4671
14.	108	475	246	150	249	3054	1197
15.	170	0	792	248	68	4035	6965
16.	392	224	592	168	0	1024	5340
17.	112	544	0	128	426	1592	0
18.	0	371	432	118	0	1278	0
19.	459	0	164	343	595	5382	834
20.	72	585	0	384	0	938	1452
21.	426	152	30	702	210	519	1236
22.	360	0	207	472	623	2376	678
23.	294	76	438	414	260	7336	4896
24.	285	0	130	210	600	0	4350
25.	0	110	774	312	450	0	5832
26.	78	112	0	420	378	2604	2448
27.	154	10	249	60	0	840	3870
28.	196	600	222	132	276	560	5220
29.	588	144	114	549	154	4893	6160
30.	124	280	0	106	192	5856	1950
31.	62	95	74	42	0	420	0
32.	600	680	280	0	558	2896	1575
33.	378	175	400	176	728	311	0
34.	819	82	469	680	448	5516	984
35.	30	295	135	217	400	0	4296
36.	318	336	86	230	156	5558	5552
37.	336	306	51	85	136	482	2280
38.	144	238	408	495	192	4977	3270
39.	765	792	96	192	273	540	1050
40.	64	192	72	76	0	7758	103
41.	702	0	264	544	592	1491	1656
42.	414	53	112	152	130	2625	1584

ANSWERS

8	9	10	11	12	13	14
1. 1176	1. 1592	1. 3168	1. 0	1. 3104	1. 2376	1. 1545
2. 5292	2. 1792	2. 238	2. 6930	2. 2632	2. 6960	2. 2010
3. 4902	3. 4278	3. 976	3. 4400	3. 4081	3. 1830	3. 2172
4. 180	4. 7119	4. 500	4. 0	4. 5400	4. 2940	4. 2760
5. 1977	5. 1530	5. 798	5. 5866	5. 3528	5. 1944	5. 2875
6. 3339	6. 6399	6. 1320	6. 0	6. 4842	6. 1634	6. 0
7. 2610	7. 1312	7. 2484	7. 6248	7. 8271	7. 7065	7. 0
8. 468	8. 5152	8. 1290	8. 640	8. 865	8. 1768	8. 5124
9. 1784	9. 925	9. 1456	9. 3052	9. 0	9. 2904	9. 3144
10. 1760	10. 4160	10. 5352	10. 912	10. 763	10. 4790	10. 6776
11. 688	11. 4824	11. 6456	11. 2706	11. 5283	11. 386	11. 6118
12. 1218	12. 2769	12. 0	12. 1944	12. 999	12. 3942	12. 0
13. 4245	13. 945	13. 3150	13. 4416	13. 4347	13. 0	13. 453
14. 926	14. 7456	14. 0	14. 1068	14. 324	14. 1616	14. 0
15. 1464	15. 2178	15. 1808	15. 6314	15. 508	15. 2781	15. 0
16. 6354	16. 2055	16. 0	16. 0	16. 414	16. 0	16. 472
17. 242	17. 110	17. 3087	17. 2169	17. 2727	17. 6327	17. 638
18. 2305	18. 1886	18. 1688	18. 4186	18. 765	18. 4592	18. 0
19. 2751	19. 664	19. 8496	19. 1755	19. 888	19. 3056	19. 1491
20. 699	20. 4992	20. 5346	20. 7758	20. 556	20. 4955	20. 774
21. 2856	21. 5862	21. 2574	21. 555	21. 7408	21. 4319	21. 5728
22. 913	22. 523	22. 303	22. 1910	22. 4062	22. 4150	22. 394
23. 6468	23. 2940	23. 6909	23. 1491	23. 0	23. 1075	23. 2700
24. 7040	24. 5848	24. 1860	24. 890	24. 1928	24. 0	24. 416
25. 2725	25. 0	25. 0	25. 771	25. 2952	25. 1206	25. 900
26. 1260	26. 2313	26. 3576	26. 789	26. 3848	26. 5054	26. 4920
27. 1647	27. 5064	27. 4257	27. 721	27. 2529	27. 1473	27. 804
28. 1018	28. 3000	28. 148	28. 5202	28. 345	28. 4655	28. 4356
29. 5634	29. 5715	29. 951	29. 1830	29. 2721	29. 6080	29. 348
30. 2274	30. 6813	30. 3663	30. 1005	30. 7768	30. 5661	30. 5931
31. 0	31. 2605	31. 739	31. 1632	31. 6072	31. 2952	31. 2440
32. 3000	32. 1242	32. 7360	32. 0	32. 8397	32. 3965	32. 773
33. 1670	33. 1422	33. 4785	33. 6937	33. 4698	33. 748	33. 184
34. 728	34. 518	34. 3564	34. 7760	34. 924	34. 0	34. 3620
35. 884	35. 7281	35. 1285	35. 0	35. 7304	35. 4683	35. 764
36. 1598	36. 1214	36. 3258	36. 3795	36. 375	36. 774	36. 8109
37. 1854	37. 0	37. 4465	37. 680	37. 6651	37. 1400	37. 5364
38. 3984	38. 4068	38. 1125	38. 0	38. 6853	38. 1467	38. 4308
39. 1908	39. 7080	39. 3840	39. 2334	39. 0	39. 5368	39. 3024
40. 535	40. 1420	40. 6876	40. 5704	40. 4314	40. 2436	40. 4689
41. 1668	41. 1519	41. 3882	41. 2124	41. 6560	41. 3580	41. 2904
42. 1856	42. 1542	42. 3794	42. 951	42. 2156	42. 3732	42. 4319

ANSWERS

	15	16	17	18	19	20	21
1.	3213	2240	2268	5301	1836	1269	1890
2.	4050	902	5568	6764	2158	341	610
3.	1011	4320	396	2992	651	660	2400
4.	5832	3672	3564	627	228	3542	4136
5.	8352	3969	3840	1357	6076	6384	5874
6.	2505	1782	630	6232	3040	2988	728
7.	4566	1260	594	5568	3995	2201	2523
8.	1925	2442	540	1694	3496	2581	5368
9.	0	1770	5451	4697	3666	2508	5796
10.	7722	250	2100	2576	6715	1377	1558
11.	936	1035	4020	3496	2014	3660	5828
12.	6853	3648	1470	1155	8366	3280	798
13.	3332	4074	4982	936	3772	3168	2555
14.	6856	6715	360	1845	855	2660	1440
15.	0	3630	6240	1428	3575	2175	1600
16.	978	4048	3195	3136	8624	1691	1806
17.	960	3432	2214	960	2000	3663	450
18.	626	2376	2314	3780	3276	2268	3154
19.	8217	3294	1540	1139	969	4480	1750
20.	2776	6390	2814	770	253	8550	6764
21.	4100	858	5698	832	1485	2701	3864
22.	620	1872	1848	1088	2775	6557	230
23.	2920	1190	1716	578	4182	5304	5280
24.	1472	4399	1890	1518	3528	830	810
25.	2230	420	576	2881	1479	2430	1593
26.	3084	630	4410	1848	1891	4042	990
27.	2896	2368	3116	2052	1264	3654	8256
28.	663	7056	4130	882	2209	1079	5530
29.	456	902	2812	1246	3266	4661	2494
30.	556	1155	4482	2205	3575	1035	4104
31.	5874	2997	1536	2548	3840	3441	4757
32.	2960	464	1800	4165	5828	2145	2397
33.	2772	3519	252	1275	3403	500	5133
34.	522	520	1566	1003	3844	528	6390
35.	795	2392	5264	2457	3872	1950	6724
36.	4368	1512	660	3481	1312	4422	979
37.	2970	4056	3569	4356	1422	1173	459
38.	897	1368	3026	817	180	6020	3630
39.	578	6499	2100	1014	1224	819	1743
40.	837	680	6873	1200	5548	589	2444
41.	2295	1232	6240	1440	3145	2736	2144
42.	4424	516	2511	1620	2814	1386	768

ANSWERS

	22	23	24	25	26	27	28
1.	3520	767	714	5400	6	7	4
2.	825	792	912	1302	4	6	6
3.	1617	4320	1273	3102	4	2	2
4.	2100	4070	7084	5796	1	4	8
5.	6305	4560	600	854	5	3	3
6.	1720	924	1204	1600	5	6	5
7.	3872	1066	720	2093	2	9	6
8.	1139	2888	767	756	2	4	5
9.	1053	1350	1460	1045	2	3	5
10.	192	2670	2562	1584	1	1	4
11.	8004	975	1800	3441	2	2	8
12.	1560	1260	1152	2223	5	7	7
13.	6225	1666	2560	4420	3	10	8
14.	4510	954	2303	1400	9	8	3
15.	1188	6391	5840	1738	9	1	5
16.	1725	2241	6016	3432	3	6	2
17.	6600	968	1476	6138	6	5	9
18.	3600	4641	3960	3599	3	4	4
19.	2392	2886	4947	3596	5	8	7
20.	1144	4582	6510	3168	6	6	8
21.	1216	2695	744	1886	8	6	3
22.	6794	440	2665	6290	9	3	10
23.	5544	315	1457	648	6	7	2
24.	1968	882	1856	840	1	2	3
25.	2610	1587	3481	4392	1	7	2
26.	3492	525	2600	9016	4	9	4
27.	1500	6408	558	2592	3	4	1
28.	5292	2697	6633	4611	5	5	7
29.	484	2002	864	4590	2	8	5
30.	4234	1250	1248	2914	8	3	6
31.	3920	1892	2349	2100	2	14	6
32.	2244	2660	2542	616	4	3	2
33.	2850	1898	273	2597	7	3	9
34.	900	539	6552	2860	3	5	7
35.	2967	1887	3068	1273	3	3	2
36.	5005	1944	3300	1943	3	9	1
37.	2548	3388	375	1953	2	4	9
38.	253	572	7623	1254	8	9	2
39.	910	3198	1312	3230	7	8	9
40.	4455	2679	1710	2100	4	5	6
41.	403	912	1664	1008	5	4	7
42.	3534	1040	1876	2016	5	8	4

ANSWERS

	29	30	31	32	33	34	35
1.	7	5	5	10	4	9	6
2.	5	6	8	9	7	7	7
3.	1	8	3	3	4	6	5
4.	5	4	2	6	9	8	5
5.	5	5	5	4	7	6	8
6.	2	5	4	10	3	9	6
7.	1	8	2	4	9	4	9
8.	9	6	6	7	3	8	3
9.	3	9	5	8	6	3	6
10.	3	3	1	5	1	8	4
11.	3	1	1	3	9	6	7
12.	6	6	7	6	1	10	2
13.	5	3	5	9	4	3	4
14.	9	11	3	11	8	6	7
15.	1	3	7	6	6	1	3
16.	3	9	3	6	1	2	5
17.	6	3	5	3	9	4	4
18.	8	10	3	12	1	2	7
19.	8	4	4	9	9	9	2
20.	8	3	8	2	4	7	4
21.	8	6	4	4	12	3	4
22.	4	9	7	18	7	9	6
23.	6	3	2	6	6	7	6
24.	1	9	7	2	2	4	6
25.	7	1	4	2	6	3	7
26.	4	7	8	9	7	5	9
27.	2	5	6	3	4	7	3
28.	9	7	6	6	8	1	1
29.	2	3	7	5	5	7	9
30.	2	4	9	7	8	3	7
31.	7	2	7	4	1	2	2
32.	4	3	4	4	6	6	8
33.	9	4	2	5	5	5	11
34.	7	4	1	7	1	1	6
35.	5	4	4	8	7	4	5
36.	3	2	8	2	8	2	3
37.	3	7	2	4	2	1	9
38.	9	2	3	9	5	9	2
39.	7	1	4	9	6	4	1
40.	2	1	1	1	5	7	3
41.	9	9	4	6	2	8	8
42.	3	8	6	2	3	7	5

ANSWERS

	36	37	38	39	40	41	42
1.	19	51	54	49	80	79	17
2.	52	37	15	77	92	43	99
3.	26	73	85	51	86	3	4
4.	17	63	10	16	21	94	26
5.	83	55	38	65	43	38	37
6.	60	12	12	94	61	4	5
7.	24	30	99	32	13	81	62
8.	72	29	18	53	12	91	84
9.	75	52	62	48	36	3	2
10.	89	57	14	11	34	44	18
11.	98	54	40	14	82	73	104
12.	20	78	78	79	39	5	8
13.	34	35	17	39	60	84	66
14.	94	71	58	88	41	80	89
15.	36	70	62	31	76	3	1
16.	73	64	61	77	25	13	40
17.	79	33	69	59	32	49	49
18.	73	93	49	99	47	34	59
19.	62	77	42	54	28	4	7
20.	65	74	23	41	40	25	57
21.	16	12	80	87	71	50	91
22.	43	51	21	95	53	84	41
23.	74	83	49	54	55	5	3
24.	46	21	39	64	51	76	28
25.	21	29	10	94	18	76	38
26.	38	136	19	57	29	31	68
27.	54	92	59	55	68	6	7
28.	97	68	13	22	59	99	27
29.	23	37	67	87	65	79	46
30.	52	19	86	94	84	69	50
31.	16	17	21	84	66	3	2
32.	72	13	54	32	98	64	91
33.	26	21	51	84	70	67	96
34.	28	12	46	97	77	1	2
35.	44	90	76	16	24	13	17
36.	59	26	76	73	91	39	62

ANSWERS

	43	44	45	46	47	48	49
1.	73	28	51	85	84	61	27
2.	99	72	23	3	4	31	39
3.	1	6	3	28	63	51	40
4.	40	88	39	6	3	23	16
5.	57	30	44	12	56	97	10
6.	2	9	3	5	9	19	19
7.	31	36	52	59	54	79	83
8.	12	53	53	2	2	18	26
9.	4	8	5	14	32	32	13
10.	75	27	71	4	8	11	13
11.	78	85	46	89	81	89	44
12.	7	5	2	4	6	48	37
13.	58	24	42	28	56	44	70
14.	46	29	29	6	5	25	19
15.	5	4	4	48	49	24	16
16.	51	25	23	2	6	48	10
17.	44	89	50	69	91	41	85
18.	41	84	57	8	4	50	58
19.	7	4	2	42	48	36	60
20.	62	69	10	5	6	60	48
21.	82	39	37	97	56	45	78
22.	83	66	23	7	9	19	20
23.	7	2	4	80	81	78	89
24.	65	85	67	2	7	17	19
25.	27	31	57	76	83	40	67
26.	38	41	94	6	16	63	12
27.	6	8	6	86	52	50	79
28.	87	12	53	8	44	37	78
29.	17	60	55	16	61	10	50
30.	16	26	25	9	81	12	31
31.	3	6	5	74	94	56	60
32.	71	56	87	7	11	42	39
33.	25	51	26	89	73	68	64
34.	6	3	7	5	67	14	29
35.	70	24	50	58	93	60	26
36.	47	19	53	49	35	53	38

ANSWERS

	50	51	52	53	54	55	56
1.	17	1489	330	786	108	4485	174
2.	34	15	81	206	1732	2888	121
3.	67	114	112	5187	107	88	1383
4.	12	1504	1618	860	2142	796	758
5.	43	167	118	2150	86	452	3710
6.	67	4575	1554	1316	206	1307	361
7.	12	40	75	3420	75	728	1021
8.	29	321	783	242	1612	1792	128
9.	99	112	638	4408	1055	95	2220
10.	12	7084	236	1111	210	46	362
11.	86	325	182	73	45	388	419
12.	24	704	672	110	360	113	5616
13.	49	270	884	446	1512	3654	45
14.	56	226	308	68	3234	445	1604
15.	49	80	216	884	149	492	663
16.	14	1151	264	175	46	464	54
17.	96	555	715	2156	651	534	602
18.	25	73	5100	1137	4347	102	770
19.	35	433	1562	76	4029	114	43
20.	55	18	4187	832	115	254	1068
21.	46	2808	2080	195	571	154	1102
22.	15	1516	1735	525	95	1214	2015
23.	34	1615	31	16	156	63	401
24.	16	5520	1518	1111	1898	680	1140
25.	92	1396	289	560	1167	4508	273
26.	73	198	1171	126	455	101	1306
27.	33	542	920	2040	100	127	4347
28.	68	1061	396	806	459	1250	994
29.	75	48	763	5016	195	4655	62
30.	55	51	40	27	3182	1057	608
31.	97	353	3224	479	111	2304	417
32.	23	19	229	13	142	183	414
33.	94	107	2136	401	519	400	1139
34.	21	1466	746	1078	22	880	63
35.	81	2520	162	238	4416	370	1716
36.	51	1124	31	146	898	180	364
37.		571	3575	57	934	847	1577
38.		926	194	1097	75	7568	386
39.		2178	1870	40	1019	202	142
40.		750	637	559	940	1177	257
41.		8918	135	647	80	1255	126
42.		195	224	573	61	38	92

ANSWERS

	57	58	59	60	61	62	63
1.	1402	139	613	1061	637	100	6935
2.	1672	91	1887	345	106	58	94
3.	696	319	3720	313	327	173	1115
4.	5244	281	45	65	59	795	411
5.	619	92	1069	1251	3822	101	172
6.	348	509	2666	6097	115	1166	836
7.	1185	767	1717	99	1599	428	3510
8.	271	367	372	988	272	1600	1292
9.	416	2160	1163	72	494	358	95
10.	54	572	87	1072	1350	770	3249
11.	684	979	10	122	4620	4524	708
12.	274	702	128	379	588	1826	383
13.	912	3465	260	1920	595	901	56
14.	1398	599	1586	72	2059	515	976
15.	39	26	2295	1219	1350	246	23
16.	42	736	33	4453	42	114	1241
17.	233	73	736	794	2940	370	1540
18.	1216	3145	4263	1510	27	316	1303
19.	108	646	55	1231	529	49	259
20.	322	68	1475	22	91	61	519
21.	1262	751	558	199	1290	20	35
22.	46	103	816	1718	760	1960	1126
23.	1054	104	230	519	988	343	389
24.	1710	959	53	353	3567	531	45
25.	63	60	1361	993	542	6882	1182
26.	92	1030	70	338	33	233	77
27.	587	1116	3212	131	268	52	119
28.	792	135	135	1080	35	770	672
29.	7802	2660	307	861	64	2310	6052
30.	930	273	119	49	1733	107	20
31.	82	2914	2340	315	93	1355	6
32.	14	20	403	1188	581	700	5610
33.	6660	1860	2967	791	1791	1348	26
34.	7626	1390	49	3477	156	1242	1196
35.	1292	786	283	2888	1078	170	5952
36.	211	1610	108	76	605	1827	337
37.	149	650	900	1437	1101	242	406
38.	312	2496	1305	666	38	48	460
39.	463	14	347	89	41	2201	226
40.	898	1521	3626	31	127	1665	467
41.	203	40	523	98	5762	504	1320
42.	663	1048	2280	407	296	5544	90

ANSWERS

	64	65	66	67	68	69	70
1.	537	36	89	884	3111	794	197
2.	6241	4760	204	651	85	530	1339
3.	104	1042	2624	762	403	3666	77
4.	86	122	794	7482	5893	1290	349
5.	539	1153	143	2280	1794	569	103
6.	74	229	1805	285	1049	57	417
7.	1740	109	511	54	178	52	445
8.	38	1565	793	1036	495	92	1076
9.	682	210	41	678	467	8648	2993
10.	3721	840	98	2565	463	895	475
11.	504	1134	314	124	568	211	109
12.	1059	104	2280	870	1104	120	646
13.	183	219	80	8190	4814	3280	1397
14.	1354	1638	781	2275	146	83	1702
15.	768	192	2288	54	1170	78	4814
16.	1908	103	717	303	2068	1156	3700
17.	7482	1003	525	360	1501	40	805
18.	483	1060	47	93	7144	1062	9
19.	43	563	1349	159	1105	1298	336
20.	646	1420	55	88	1420	95	543
21.	383	7008	5135	113	78	253	960
22.	1387	14	820	1092	32	1047	34
23.	300	6048	1138	264	56	286	660
24.	351	3479	43	764	3871	2940	25
25.	2555	673	23	1628	446	1664	46
26.	40	109	2881	377	277	2790	68
27.	944	115	131	1790	1830	1070	1113
28.	84	587	629	103	100	1277	89
29.	150	2350	8448	419	1210	199	500
30.	1894	75	123	101	489	1584	13
31.	17	212	559	2590	27	2993	282
32.	605	4940	506	1922	9408	175	3422
33.	1422	1099	1890	795	396	15	203
34.	529	345	5952	75	124	2560	1134
35.	59	28	946	242	324	682	1423
36.	667	100	1457	4968	430	118	1040
37.	1222	60	1760	1742	101	1322	5460
38.	975	1178	1246	195	264	939	1315
39.	129	877	42	1680	2365	68	2400
40.	82	400	2961	670	6290	4560	31
41.	1485	927	82	88	1675	1508	1155
42.	804	38	414	71	316	3	793

ANSWERS

	71	72	73	74	75	76	77
1.	4416	479	1089	76	1242	624	166
2.	17	1171	55	1830	543	94	1662
3.	1598	20	727	768	1717	1539	289
4.	217	658	29	80	347	18	39
5.	438	119	458	43	129	185	371
6.	1680	1950	659	2688	1303	89	143
7.	748	179	1922	3100	891	966	405
8.	1340	758	340	45	420	454	255
9.	85	4026	171	829	79	2666	3476
10.	192	731	129	239	1734	70	1337
11.	5200	1079	2961	1612	1058	133	22
12.	537	312	8	122	387	3864	377
13.	1040	2024	141	357	1037	139	578
14.	1530	241	33	15	709	930	1827
15.	726	551	1435	37	832	215	168
16.	1115	65	81	1020	5220	407	412
17.	624	2660	143	188	36	317	756
18.	1420	457	5184	52	621	698	1080
19.	454	2160	4189	7954	2	105	40
20.	369	290	731	569	174	103	936
21.	183	422	505	485	264	1133	3484
22.	330	1827	1037	1168	106	1437	2418
23.	746	210	331	150	17	1976	1510
24.	25	1480	622	2080	2880	776	663
25.	1980	206	552	2573	1172	3367	39
26.	1470	1479	5609	2968	827	4576	364
27.	1204	2736	834	30	2262	365	104
28.	68	94	15	2660	4214	869	394
29.	23	38	1232	100	2485	50	1104
30.	40	123	3813	1029	151	772	138
31.	780	18	488	769	808	28	1577
32.	846	1213	1273	1351	288	924	578
33.	33	109	1221	167	691	589	5046
34.	916	748	66	851	1587	158	5025
35.	558	816	1450	106	147	3266	845
36.	408	527	61	6083	1170	573	135
37.	1048	101	59	545	1320	93	35
38.	63	495	5916	1023	152	248	1034
39.	991	1196	1613	337	31	122	1377
40.	318	3916	668	41	2112	1141	2744
41.	75	1014	133	4380	172	880	39
42.	3071	97	36	1109	63	469	5130

ANSWERS

78	79	80	81	82	83	84
1. 4233	1. 199	1. 224	1. 11	1. 313	1. 531	1. 65
2. 3763	2. 504	2. 1440	2. 261	2. 37	2. 1639	2. 925
3. 158	3. 1292	3. 84	3. 5184	3. 492	3. 633	3. 189
4. 7636	4. 211	4. 1097	4. 1412	4. 616	4. 1787	4. 119
5. 269	5. 29	5. 1752	5. 1199	5. 749	5. 4757	5. 337
6. 1831	6. 2686	6. 126	6. 1764	6. 1414	6. 996	6. 1173
7. 42	7. 30	7. 114	7. 1863	7. 1803	7. 2574	7. 228
8. 3008	8. 92	8. 1185	8. 412	8. 900	8. 1221	8. 479
9. 244	9. 881	9. 41	9. 1379	9. 166	9. 2130	9. 192
10. 665	10. 3876	10. 1100	10. 290	10. 884	10. 378	10. 39
11. 163	11. 36	11. 274	11. 853	11. 6438	11. 256	11. 2059
12. 26	12. 972	12. 873	12. 467	12. 109	12. 12	12. 1530
13. 135	13. 488	13. 2890	13. 3160	13. 1271	13. 1078	13. 155
14. 1887	14. 503	14. 179	14. 861	14. 2112	14. 176	14. 469
15. 55	15. 651	15. 1363	15. 51	15. 254	15. 567	15. 96
16. 960	16. 752	16. 156	16. 990	16. 1468	16. 1581	16. 2430
17. 2232	17. 254	17. 113	17. 30	17. 2220	17. 2208	17. 1714
18. 1005	18. 82	18. 3752	18. 270	18. 1053	18. 1182	18. 521
19. 196	19. 416	19. 1368	19. 61	19. 73	19. 313	19. 82
20. 594	20. 747	20. 98	20. 1711	20. 426	20. 108	20. 1634
21. 26	21. 1464	21. 591	21. 146	21. 78	21. 504	21. 300
22. 184	22. 2976	22. 990	22. 1130	22. 861	22. 943	22. 390
23. 66	23. 1092	23. 1315	23. 121	23. 438	23. 2494	23. 5589
24. 3950	24. 106	24. 692	24. 591	24. 39	24. 1140	24. 2132
25. 950	25. 1127	25. 5775	25. 907	25. 120	25. 70	25. 737
26. 6308	26. 1600	26. 205	26. 258	26. 1428	26. 267	26. 131
27. 28	27. 468	27. 62	27. 277	27. 410	27. 19	27. 2550
28. 201	28. 1701	28. 809	28. 65	28. 96	28. 1297	28. 453
29. 333	29. 4224	29. 588	29. 829	29. 29	29. 93	29. 312
30. 2940	30. 2256	30. 672	30. 52	30. 218	30. 251	30. 6272
31. 1705	31. 1705	31. 200	31. 4686	31. 576	31. 158	31. 1068
32. 94	32. 697	32. 200	32. 4371	32. 35	32. 178	32. 416
33. 16	33. 1153	33. 1628	33. 82	33. 2204	33. 936	33. 72
34. 344	34. 32	34. 389	34. 1848	34. 1806	34. 676	34. 41
35. 356	35. 1496	35. 62	35. 119	35. 83	35. 5040	35. 550
36. 1381	36. 138	36. 4900	36. 73	36. 857	36. 588	36. 114
37. 934	37. 1054	37. 2808	37. 155	37. 1980	37. 62	37. 109
38. 840	38. 696	38. 5490	38. 3744	38. 35	38. 6762	38. 155
39. 1053	39. 72	39. 166	39. 1002	39. 142	39. 46	39. 1527
40. 1128	40. 1797	40. 633	40. 288	40. 1170	40. 851	40. 8736
41. 214	41. 467	41. 357	41. 5880	41. 17	41. 40	41. 1603
42. 63	42. 1361	42. 813	42. 31	42. 341	42. 1	42. 636

ANSWERS

	85	86	87	88	89	90	91
1.	131	532	220	989	716	5394	608
2.	47	139	663	67	324	155	87
3.	1025	231	811	4851	336	537	792
4.	121	157	149	392	491	24	105
5.	1932	1632	204	4032	964	1298	1760
6.	92	483	58	163	972	15	963
7.	205	95	5152	59	6308	533	46
8.	82	117	3306	1716	1848	257	1014
9.	500	3696	1331	1017	111	435	195
10.	1474	23	124	340	60	521	1150
11.	12	52	23	1275	707	2624	135
12.	4116	498	1020	1211	1268	2000	1554
13.	2430	2744	1044	1262	88	121	25
14.	2842	71	3721	262	41	2442	112
15.	642	45	108	7392	302	5859	6499
16.	3196	6351	650	48	2700	139	1294
17.	1436	680	99	468	6468	623	4720
18.	218	264	746	1472	210	415	127
19.	1440	706	719	1274	102	16	670
20.	492	883	1235	311	150	898	422
21.	1700	153	1290	418	646	2640	168
22.	852	6030	4464	22	2365	958	74
23.	5256	442	3626	111	409	236	3450
24.	908	21	1637	1295	6636	473	479
25.	3201	1221	43	300	524	94	45
26.	663	2295	90	1037	3813	1342	3666
27.	149	444	732	96	1056	17	118
28.	434	1878	23	29	53	5544	81
29.	849	365	324	1914	3	1341	468
30.	46	27	1567	453	2976	4345	74
31.	713	2790	2852	6570	459	132	6794
32.	140	531	44	770	713	1195	56
33.	104	440	870	25	1140	39	298
34.	35	103	121	252	1012	835	490
35.	276	770	97	1624	110	195	609
36.	305	1109	194	303	10	194	2736
37.	89	100	257	450	916	1185	102
38.	347	1103	414	560	19	89	5073
39.	40	1092	2646	113	179	1095	1024
40.	2550	783	239	123	1670	53	3139
41.	962	547	97	6450	349	464	846
42.	1722	821	215	175	298	183	711

ANSWERS

	92	93	94	95	96	97	98
1.	57	529	1126	459	920	7134	1372
2.	317	2380	237	1704	1614	51	1689
3.	171	41	140	3348	447	345	103
4.	4185	419	1320	34	800	828	1623
5.	15	1273	108	1020	444	84	1771
6.	1056	3621	48	84	276	364	108
7.	19	330	2964	516	2108	266	1149
8.	450	118	74	118	638	629	486
9.	3731	7505	2444	958	186	1856	3420
10.	706	1058	15	571	1260	1584	16
11.	5304	293	763	107	1623	1176	840
12.	164	85	1776	300	324	7	992
13.	3243	564	1282	511	1730	15	57
14.	1639	1209	1364	59	1440	214	619
15.	1122	155	484	307	185	5589	34
16.	5226	116	800	1308	407	852	169
17.	95	730	322	662	43	90	26
18.	442	80	1364	147	1425	1132	22
19.	738	81	127	76	13	695	2499
20.	255	3139	1190	98	68	103	49
21.	4131	378	242	462	274	946	405
22.	78	50	87	185	822	51	34
23.	42	63	1012	1294	1679	2128	3094
24.	399	1840	985	211	1722	6450	3675
25.	774	94	42	506	405	544	1232
26.	985	1283	320	4320	43	978	39
27.	83	1477	554	50	743	107	162
28.	47	1938	1343	1227	196	1333	80
29.	89	1070	1548	483	149	124	449
30.	214	1083	291	1493	624	76	137
31.	1150	5254	592	1289	27	1220	771
32.	1170	35	73	1028	1260	639	163
33.	910	1083	1334	34	3068	88	473
34.	1702	640	2324	908	1156	124	240
35.	843	49	292	1360	23	850	3577
36.	232	193	95	113	788	1256	436
37.	43	444	128	101	3741	13	144
38.	5600	179	88	118	1017	1062	1585
39.	233	966	1371	5192	315	2601	68
40.	963	1275	1788	420	896	388	124
41.	314	166	154	31	118	132	2668
42.	466	169	6	2891	186	39	3348

ANSWERS

99	100
1. 1139	1. 261
2. 321	2. 1065
3. 31	3. 87
4. 279	4. 1092
5. 1369	5. 1364
6. 23	6. 53
7. 97	7. 181
8. 80	8. 195
9. 1191	9. 55
10. 116	10. 5270
11. 1818	11. 1971
12. 3515	12. 3300
13. 2166	13. 633
14. 1795	14. 530
15. 81	15. 506
16. 31	16. 112
17. 126	17. 114
18. 116	18. 2120
19. 6900	19. 3600
20. 23	20. 116
21. 1541	21. 104
22. 802	22. 355
23. 165	23. 1224
24. 165	24. 1890
25. 980	25. 1417
26. 3596	26. 70
27. 4032	27. 3042
28. 1035	28. 658
29. 900	29. 545
30. 1421	30. 226
31. 1550	31. 127
32. 84	32. 1801
33. 255	33. 73
34. 72	34. 1315
35. 98	35. 100
36. 1242	36. 1824
37. 1130	37. 2256
38. 183	38. 636
39. 95	39. 1449
40. 163	40. 765
41. 3450	41. 3854
42. 51	42. 280

Manufactured by Amazon.ca
Bolton, ON

28374317R00066